Exodus: Called Out

T. C. HADDEN

Copyright 2017 by T.C. Hadden.
The book author retains sole copyright to his contributions to this book.

Published 2017.
Printed in the United States of America.

All rights reserved.

No portion of this book may be reproduced, stored in a retrieval system, or transmitted in any form or by any means – electronic, mechanical, photocopy, recording, scanning, or other – except for brief quotations in critical reviews or articles, without the prior written permission of the author.

ISBN 978-1-946234-13-1
Front cover design by Mark Gauthier.

This book was published by BookCrafters, Parker, Colorado.
bookcrafterscolorado@gmail.com

This book may be ordered from www.bookcrafters.net and other online bookstores.

Foreword

Thank you for selecting this volume of the Expository series. These volumes are the contribution of various Apostolic writers. Their biography is on the back cover. The publishers of the Expository series would like to extend a thank you for helping us get this valuable material into the hands of readers.

The desire is that people would read the scriptures and be blessed. These commentary works, or works of Expository subjects, will give insight to, and further the understanding of the readers.

Each of these authors hold the values of the original Apostles of Jesus Christ. These writers want to hold to the values expostulated in the New Testament by Jesus and his disciples. Each of them ascribe to the concept offered by the Apostle John, "I have no greater joy than to hear that my children walk in truth."

Truth has been passed down through generations and has survived critics and doubters. Truth will prevail and ultimately triumph.

These writings are our contribution to the river of written truth that has flowed down through the ages.

Read and be blessed.

Kenneth Bow

Preface

Exodus: Called Out was a labor of intense time, research, and painstaking care to develop a word-based commentary that not only focused upon the historical-cultural context, but the language of the text. Too often, Old Testament exegesis is the victim of biased and subjective interpretation where a degree of reading backwards into the text informs one's own doctrines and opinions. That being said, Exodus: Called Out is meant to allow for a naturally unfolding revelation of the events, actions, and narrative of the nation of Israel as they moved out of Egypt and began their journey toward Canaan. I am sure, as time progresses, that future revisions will be released to allow for the correction of grammatical errors missed at this first publishing. I am very thankful for the opportunity that Ken Bow has provided in allowing for an easy process of publishing and will forever remain grateful for his encouragement to do this. Please note that chapters 35-40 are not included in this commentary due to the nature of the chapters in that they merely summarize the nature of the Tabernacle of God being built and reiterate the prior commandments already given in earlier chapters.

Introduction

Serving as a continuation of Genesis, the book of Exodus moves one from the development of God's promises given to Abraham, including the foretold servitude Abraham's seed would endure, to the birth of a covenant nation. The narrative, beginning with the bondage of Israel and culminating with the erection of the Tabernacle, reveals a new epoch that sets the tone for future Biblical history and the development of the nation of Israel. In the book of Genesis, individual men were found to garner the attention and commission of God whereas in Exodus, God's attention turns toward His firstborn son (the nation of Israel), as the generation of inheritance, that is commissioned to receive the geographical promises given to Abraham. With this transition, God moves from a transcendent Divine power to one that is engaged in relational motif's that encompass both cultural and familial ideas, such as, a Suzerain Lord, father, and even, a friend. Exodus introduces several key Biblical components such as the Tabernacle, the Sabbath, the Ten Commandments, as well as other moral and ritual laws, and various concepts that would serve as foreshadows of redemption.

Authorship

Internal evidence suggests that Exodus was written and compiled by Moses (cf. Ex. 17:14; 24:4) and external evidence, ranging from Davidic reference to the Apostle Paul, commonly refer to the "words" or the "law of Moses" (cf. I Kin. 2:3; Rom. 10:5). Jesus Himself would reference Exodus 20:12 with the introduction of "For Moses said," (Mark 7:10; cf. Luke 20:37), lending even more support to the identify of Moses as the author of Exodus.

Historical Setting:

The approximate dates of the events in the Book of Exodus are speculative, with many scholars holding to 13th century model that ranges from 1267-1290 B.C. However, scriptural evidence indicates otherwise. According to I Kings 6:1, Solomon began to build the temple in the fourth year of his reign, 480 years after the children of Israel came out of Egypt. By adding this figure to the well-substantiated fourth year of Solomon's reign (967-966) one arrives at 1447-1446 B.C, a figure that also finds further confirmation in recent archeological digs in Jericho, Ai, and Hazor. Based on this, the Exodus would have transpired during the reign of Amenhotep II (1452-1417) further verified by Talmudic references and a Jubilee cycle that corresponds perfectly with the date of 1446 B.C.

CHAPTER ONE

¹ Now these *are* the names of the children of Israel, which came into Egypt; every man and his household came with Jacob. ² Reuben, Simeon, Levi, and Judah, ³ Issachar, Zebulun, and Benjamin, ⁴ Dan, and Naphtali, Gad, and Asher.

Serving as a prelude, the introductory paragraph of Exodus marks a transition from the book of Genesis to the Book of Exodus. The emphasis of the discourse rests heavily on the process of a few becoming many, as is seen in 1:7. While Genesis dealt primarily with the *family* of Abraham, Isaac, and Jacob, Exodus would focus on the birth of a *nation*, holding to the paradigm of Abrahamic promises found throughout the Genesis narrative. **Reuben, Simeon, Levi, and Judah**: first the children of Leah are mentioned, followed by Rachel's second son (Joseph having been in Egypt already), and finally the children of the handmaidens. A full parallel account of Jacob's migration into Egypt is first detailed in Genesis 46:26-27.

⁵ **And all the souls that came out of the loins of Jacob were seventy souls: for Joseph was in Egypt *already*.**

The collective body of those who migrated into Egypt may appear complicated since several textual accounts seem to differ. In Genesis 46:26, (*sixty-six*) are said to have migrated into Egypt, but Jacob and his son's wives are not included in the number. Genesis 46:27, while including Jacob and Joseph, also adds the two sons of Joseph as well, paralleling the figure of seventy presented in Exodus 1:5. This figure (*seventy*) is again established in Deut. 10:22. Another figure, reflected in Acts 7:14 and the Septuagint, tallies the number at *seventy-five*.

⁶ And Joseph died, and all his brethren, and all that generation.

Chronological events, beginning with Genesis 41:46, reveal that Joseph was *thirty-nine* when the collective family of Jacob entered into Egypt. Joseph is recorded as having died at *110* (Gen. 50:26). This would account for 54 years that Joseph saw his grandchildren and some of his great-grandchildren (Gen. 50:23).

⁷ And the children of Israel were fruitful, and increased abundantly, and multiplied, and waxed exceeding mighty; and the land was filled with them.

Several words are used (progressive in nature) to emphasize the increase of the nation of Israel in Egypt.

1. Fruitful (cf. Gen. 1:22,28; 8:17; 9:1,7).
2. Increased abundantly (cf. Gen. 1:20,21; 7:21; 8:17; 9:7).
3. Multiplied (cf. Gen. 1:22,28; 8:17).
4. Filled the Land (cf. Gen. 1:22,28; 9:1).

Each of these four expressions find first mention in the creative narrative of Genesis 1 and also in the articulated commandments of God post-flood (Gen. 8 and 9). This would bring the reader to understand that *the progressive increase of Israel in Egypt followed the cycle of creative growth and dominion,* even while the rigors of hard labor and bondage sought to limit and diminish their numbers. It should be noted that the phrase **waxed exceeding mighty**, not listed in these expressions of increase, involves three Hebrew words, two of which (**waxed exceeding**) place a double emphasis (lit. *very, very*) upon mighty. Since Hebrew lacks punctuation, this literary technique of term repetition is often used throughout scripture to express a degree of emphasis (cf. Ezek. 37:10).

⁸ Now there arose up a new king over Egypt, which knew not Joseph.

Steven, in Acts 7:18, uses the Greek word ἕτερος (héteros) which means *another* or *different* king, implying **a king that was unlike the previous**. Probable evidence points towards a Hyksos ruler that was unfamiliar with Egyptian history or the events surrounding Joseph's rise to power. Holding to this belief, Isaiah 52:4 speaks of their Egyptian oppressors as Assyrian, agreeing with the Mesopotamian origin of the Hyksos people.

⁹ And he said unto his people, Behold, the people of the children of Israel *are* more and mightier than we: ¹⁰ Come on, let us deal wisely with them; lest they multiply, and it come to pass, that, when there falleth out any war, they join also unto our enemies, and fight against us, and so get them up out of the land. ¹¹ Therefore they did set over them taskmasters to afflict them with their burdens. And they built for Pharaoh treasure cities, Pithom and Raamses. ¹² But the

more they afflicted them, the more they multiplied and grew. And they were grieved because of the children of Israel. ¹³ **And the Egyptians made the children of Israel to serve with rigour:** ¹⁴ **And they made their lives bitter with hard bondage, in morter, and in brick, and in all manner of service in the field: all their service, wherein they made them serve,** *was* **with rigour.**

The king of Egypt, having no direct charge of wrongdoing against the Hebrews, had to **deal wisely** (lit. *cleverly*) with them **lest they multiply**. If one were to place this decree within the context of the progressive growth of the nation of Israel (vs. 7), it may have occurred while they were **increased abundantly** and before they **multiplied**. To remedy the possibility of exponential growth, Pharaoh employed a sequential series of actions against the Hebrew nation in order to suppress them, lest they **join also unto our enemies, and fight against us**. Again, this may lend toward a Hyksos ruler that was worried about the Hebrews joining with the conquered Egyptians.

The first action in the sequence was to set **taskmasters** מס(mas), meaning *forced labor or enforced levy*. It is possible that, rather than forced labor, this decree implied the latter, a form of labor equivalent to that of a feudal serfdom. Having land that was within the realm of Egyptian territory, Pharaoh began to implement a system of levy that would limit their holding while increasing his. This action would build treasure cities (lit. *storage-spaces*) in **Pithom and Raameses**, referring to large storehouses of agricultural yield (cf. II Chron. 32:28). This effort of enforced levy would do little to diminish the fruitful abundance of the Israelites and the Egyptians were **grieved** (lit. to become sick), implying that they began to loathe even the sight of the Israelites (cf. Num. 22:3, see *distressed*).

Realizing that an enforced levy did little to stem the success and growth of the Israelites, Pharaoh enacted phase two, making **their lives bitter with hard bondage** (lit. *harshness or cruelty*). Ordinary labor with an enforced levy transitioned to a **work of rigour**, a word whose Hebraic stem signifies "*to break apart.*" This phase **made their lives bitter**, something that would be remembered in every Passover feast in the future (cf. Ex. 12:8). Once again though, despite the bitterness of crushing labor, one sees the implied ineffectiveness of this tactic to diminish the fruitful growth of the nation of Israel, thus a more direct approach is taken as Pharaoh initiates a third phase of oppression.

¹⁵ And the king of Egypt spake to the Hebrew midwives, of which the name of the one *was* Shiphrah, and the name of the other Puah: ¹⁶ And he said, When ye do the office of a midwife to the Hebrew women, and see *them* upon the stools; if it be a son, then ye shall kill him: but if it *be* a daughter, then she shall live.

Speaking to two of the chief administrators of the many midwives, the king entered the third phase of oppression. He commands the midwives to kill each Hebrew child that was perceived as male when seen **upon the stools** (lit. *two stones*), the birthstone seat that women, in a squatting position, gave labour upon. The word used here (**stools**) הָאׇבְנָיִם, (*'obĕnayim*), is the same word used in Jeremiah 18:3 for the *potter's wheel* where clay is fashioned and brought to definition. Since mention of such birthing stools are not associated with later Israelite birth it may be plausible that the birthing stones played a significant role in Egyptian superstitions and customs as it related to child birth and their notions of creation. Nevertheless, what Pharaoh wished to implement was despicably evil. He was promoting an **active birth abortion** accomplished by the midwives as the children were identified when leaving the birth canal. The entire premise behind this plan was to still maintain a cloak of secrecy against the malicious intent of Pharaoh.

[17] But the midwives feared God, and did not as the king of Egypt commanded them, but saved the men children alive. [18] And the king of Egypt called for the midwives, and said unto them, Why have ye done this thing, and have saved the men children alive? [19] And the midwives said unto Pharaoh, Because the Hebrew women *are* **not as the Egyptian women; for they** *are* **lively, and are delivered ere the midwives come in unto them.**

This reason given by the midwives may certainly reflect a truthful response, rather than subterfuge. The Hebrew women are revealed to be **lively** (lit. *vigorous*) and thus, as people of hard labor and bondage, they are given to deliver in a manner that is unlike the Egyptian women. By the time the midwives arrived, perhaps even if they came slowly, the Hebrew women had already given birth. Regardless, the midwives had already decided to let the male children live before they even arrived to assist in the deliveries.

[20] Therefore God dealt well with the midwives: and the people multiplied, and waxed very mighty.

Once again, we are brought to the progressive increase of Ex. 1:7, where the Israelites **waxed exceeding mighty**.

Despite the best attempts of Pharaoh to crush the Hebrew's discreetly, the Israelites continued to not only increase numerically but also grew stronger as a people.

²¹ And it came to pass, because the midwives feared God, that he made them houses.

Some scholars believe the houses in question here are not directed toward the midwives. Instead, due to the nature of the midwives' refusal to carry out the plans of Pharaoh, he (Pharaoh) had some form of public housing built for the Israelites to ensure that the Egyptians could keep a watchful eye on the birth of every child lest any new males go unseen.

²² And Pharaoh charged all his people, saying, Every son that is born ye shall cast into the river, and every daughter ye shall save alive.

Forsaking a subtle approach, Pharaoh implements the final stage of his war against the increase of Israel by openly commanding all his people to cast every son born to the Hebrew people into the Nile River. Pharaoh, like many genocidal dictators to come, would systematically turn the citizens of Egypt against the Hebrew nation so that the charge of genocide would be taken up by those captured by fear, loathing, and prejudice against the Israelite people.

Notes

CHAPTER TWO

¹ And there went a man of the house of Levi, and took *to wife* **a daughter of Levi.**

Exodus 6:20 reveals the identity of the Levite man and woman as Amram and Jochabed. Though it seems to imply the act of marriage coincided with the genocidal decree, scripture indicates the presence of Aaron, who would have been three years old at the time of Moses' birth (cf. Ex. 7:7), as well as, Miriam, the eldest child (Ex. 2:4). Here, the emphasis is upon the conception of vs. 2, **(the woman conceived)**. In other words, at the same time of the decree of Pharaoh that **all the people** throw the Hebrew male newborns in the Nile, **Jochabed** bare a son.

² And the woman conceived, and bare a son: and when she saw him that he *was a* **goodly** *child*, **she hid him three months. ³ And when she could not longer hide him, she took for him an ark of bulrushes, and daubed it with slime and with pitch, and put the child therein; and she laid it in the flags by the river's brink. ⁴ And his sister stood afar off, to wit what would be done to him.**

A **goodly child** could imply the child's good-natured demeanor as a newborn, thus enabling Jochebed to hide him without fear of discovery. However, according to Hebrews 11:23, it was still an act of faith on the part of Amram and Jochebed when they saw Moses was a **proper** (Gk. *Asteios*), meaning comely or well-mannered, child. Being unable to hide the child more than three months, they made an **ark of bulrushes** (lit. *papyrus*) covered within and without with a natural waterproofing agent and placed it, and the child, into the river near to the **flags** (the *reeds*). It should be noted, contrary to many accounts that envision the ark being tossed in the strong currents of the Nile River overpopulated by crocodiles, that the ark was placed along the *edge of the river among the reeds*. This action would keep the ark from moving downstream.

Remarkably, when considering Miriam's task of awaiting **what would be done to him**, it may reveal that Jochabed had planned for the daughter of Pharaoh to discover the child. More than likely, knowing the character and habits of the royal daughter, either through divine direction or human gamble, they anticipated the reaction of the royal daughter and the compassion she would exhibit upon seeing the child.

[5] **And the daughter of Pharaoh came down to wash** *herself* **at the river; and her maidens walked along by the river's side; and when she saw the ark among the flags, she sent her maid to fetch it.** [6] **And when she had opened it, she saw the child: and, behold, the babe wept. And she had compassion on him, and said, This** *is one* **of the Hebrews' children.**

Lending to the anticipated events of Jochebed, the unnamed daughter of Pharaoh and her maidens come along the edge of the river where the ark is spotted. When the royal daughter opened the ark, two things happen. First, she sees the child weeping and secondly, she immediately identifies the child as one of the Hebrew children. It is the former (weeping) that causes her to be moved with compassion toward the child, knowing full well the decree her father had issued.

[7] Then said his sister to Pharaoh's daughter, Shall I go and call to thee a nurse of the Hebrew women, that she may nurse the child for thee? [8] And Pharaoh's daughter said to her, Go. And the maid went and called the child's mother. [9] And Pharaoh's daughter said unto her, Take this child away, and nurse it for me, and I will give *thee* thy wages. And the woman took the child, and nursed it.

The sudden arrival of Miriam, a Hebrew woman, doesn't seem to alarm the royal daughter. It is likely, following the events of the narrative, that the royal daughter put two-and-two together and recognized the strategy for what it was; an attempt to save a child. Regardless of the royal daughters awareness, she was willing to use the situation to her advantage, allowing for the true mother to nurse the child for her. This is speculative at best, but it remains evident that the hand of God was in these actions.

[10] And the child grew, and she brought him unto Pharaoh's daughter, and he became her son. And she called his name Moses: and she said, Because I drew him out of the water.

A period of 2-3 years is implied, though it may have extended further. These years of weaning are the most critical in the development of the emotional, mental, physical, and social frameworks of a child's mind. As agreed, the royal daughter claimed the child as her own, calling his name Moses. In Egyptian, **Moses** means *son* which is prefaced by the phrase **he became her son**. Coincidentally, the pronunciation of the Egyptian name would also bring the Hebrew verb masa (meaning, to ***draw out***) to mind.

[11] And it came to pass in those days, when Moses was grown, that he went out unto his brethren, and looked on their burdens: and he spied an Egyptian smiting an Hebrew, one of his brethren. [12] And he looked this way and that way, and when he saw that *there was* **no man, he slew the Egyptian, and hid him in the sand.**

Fully forty years of age and learned in all the wisdom of the Egyptians (cf. Acts 7:22-23), Moses made his first *documented* foray into the region of Hebrew labor. There is an emphasis in that Moses **saw** the burden of the Hebrews and then Moses saw an Egyptian smiting a Hebrew. Some scholars imply the phrase, **he looked this way and that way**, to mean that Moses was looking for one to oppose the wrongdoing but saw no man. Moses' observation propels him from what **he sees** to what **he does**. Observation motivated action and Moses strikes and kills the offending Egyptian.

[13] And when he went out the second day, behold, two men of the Hebrews strove together: and he said to him that did the wrong, Wherefore smitest thou thy fellow? [14] And he said, Who made thee a prince and a judge

over us? intendest thou to kill me, as thou killedst the Egyptian? And Moses feared, and said, Surely this thing is known.

The following day, when confronting two Hebrew slaves engaged in a violent dispute, the response of the wrongdoer shatters Moses' perception of how the Hebrew's would receive his actions on their behalf (cf. Acts 7:25). It is interesting that the Hebrew slaves would stand by and allow the oppressive cruelty of the Egyptians against their brethren, but they would resist any implied authority from a fellow Hebrew. Ironically, in light of the rhetorical accusation of the slave, **who made thee prince and judge over us**, the process of installing a recognized structure of **princes and judges** would occur at Sinai, not far removed from this event (cf. Ex. 18:21-25).

[15] Now when Pharaoh heard this thing, he sought to slay Moses. But Moses fled from the face of Pharaoh, and dwelt in the land of Midian: and he sat down by a well.

It is interesting that Moses would come to dwell in the very land of those who had sold Joseph into Potiphar's household many years' prior (cf. Gen. 37:36). Now the tables would turn and, those (of the nation of Midian) responsible for bringing the Hebrews into Egypt, would become the dwelling for the man that would bring the Hebrews out of Egypt.

[16] Now the priest of Midian had seven daughters: and they came and drew *water*, and filled the troughs to water their father's flock. [17]

Serving as an introduction to the events that would follow, the priest called Reuel, (lit. *friend of God*), is also referred to as Jethro, a word that may have served as an honorary title meaning, ***his excellency***. (cf. Num. 10:29).

And the shepherds came and drove them away: but Moses stood up and helped them, and watered their flock.

For the first time in scripture the Hebrew verb (helped), יָשַׁע, *yāsha*, meaning **save** is used. Once again, one is drawn to the intolerance Moses has for injustice when he assists in the process of saving the seven daughters and their flock from the tyranny of the shepherds. This attribute would play well into the inevitable call to deliver Israel from Egypt.

[18] And when they came to Reuel their father, he said, How *is it that* ye are come so soon to day? [19] And they said, An Egyptian delivered us out of the hand of the shepherds, and also drew *water* enough for us, and watered the flock. [20] And he said unto his daughters, And where is he? why *is* it *that* ye have left the man? call him, that he may eat bread. [21] And Moses was content to dwell with the man: and he gave Moses Zipporah his daughter. [22] And she bare *him* a son, and he called his name Gershom: for he said, I have been a stranger in a strange land.

An Egyptian delivered us: Moses, still arrayed in the garments and attire of an Egyptian and having the accented articulation of Egypt, would have appeared thus to the seven daughters of Reuel. It should be noted that the news of the tyrannical shepherds seemed a common place issue since they are spoken of in a familiar reference and Reuel's surprise at the speed in which his daughters had returned.

Moses was content to dwell with the man: satisfied to dwell with Reuel, Moses marries one of the seven daughters, named Zipporah. At some indeterminate time, Zipporah gives birth to Moses' first child whom he names Gershom, its namesake implying the statement, **I have been a stranger in a strange land**. The naming of his son as *"stranger there"* recalls the covenant made with Abraham well-over 200 years' prior (cf. Gen. 15:30).

23 And it came to pass in process of time, that the king of Egypt died: and the children of Israel sighed by reason of the bondage, and they cried, and their cry came up unto God by reason of the bondage.

Process of time: There is a considerable amount of time occurs here as scripture moves into the transitional narrative that will introduce the calling and the commission of Moses. In sharp contrast to Moses' being **content to dwell** in Midian is the **sighing** and **cries** of the nation of Israel in bondage.

24 And God heard their groaning, and God remembered his covenant with Abraham, with Isaac, and with Jacob. 25 And God looked upon the children of Israel, and God had respect unto *them*.

Though the affliction of Abraham's seed had been foretold, so also had the set time of deliverance (Gen. 15:12-16), which here is revealed in that God remembered. The Biblical idea of God remembering is not so much a recollection of the past, but rather, *an applied focus* upon a specific aspect of history (in this case, the covenant with Abraham) *that motivates action.* There is a unique pattern of God's **progressive involvement** that is revealed in that God: heard, remembered, looked, and had respect (knew) unto them.

Notes

CHAPTER THREE

¹ **Now Moses kept the flock of Jethro his father in law, the priest of Midian: and he led the flock to the backside of the desert, and came to the mountain of God,** *even* **to Horeb.**

Now Moses kept the flock: the once court-educated Egyptian is now a shepherd in Midian, a job that was or had once been viewed with great distaste by the Egyptians (cf. Gen. 46:34). However, little did Moses realize how such a job would come to serve him in his future commission as the leader of a fledgling Israelite nation. **And he led the flock to the backside of the desert**: Usually translated as *desert*, the Hebrew word, מִדְבָּר, *midbar*, can also indicate a ***pasture*** (cf. Gen. 37:22, Job 38:26). This maintains the idea that Moses had frequented this route many times while leading the flock to green pastures. It was on an ordinary, familiar path that Moses would encounter the Theophany as he **Came to the mountain of God, Horeb**: Called here the mountain of God in anticipation of future events, Horeb is used interchangeably throughout scripture with Sinai.

² **And the angel of the LORD appeared unto him in a flame of fire out of the midst of a bush: and he looked,**

and, behold, the bush burned with fire, and the bush *was* not consumed.

The **angel**, רַאְלָמ (malʾāk), of the Lord is an expression which indicates *a visible manifestation of God*, otherwise referred to as a Theophany. In this case, God is manifested as a **flame of fire**. The manifestation of fire is often utilized in scripture to refer to the Spirit of God (cf. Ezek. 1:4). Interestingly, the **flame** לַבָּה (*labbah*) **of fire** that would be the agency of Moses' sending would be found again as a pillar, serving to give Israel light in their going (Ex. 13:21-22). The idiom of fire is also revealed in the declaration of John the Baptist regarding the one (Jesus) that would baptize with the Holy Ghost and *fire* (Matt. 3:11). This was realized on the day of Pentecost as cloven tongues like as of *fire* sat upon those whom the Spirit of God had filled (Acts 2:1-4).

In the Old Testament, the **angel of the Lord** is first mentioned in the narrative involving Ishmael and Hagar (cf. Gen. 16:11) and continues to be used throughout scripture to accomplish divine mission and purpose (cf. Gen. 16:7-13, 22:9-18; Num. 20:16, 22:22-35; Jgs. 2:1-4, 5:23, 6:11-24, 13:13-22; II Sam. 24:15-17; Zech. 1:7-17, 3:1-10).

[3] And Moses said, I will now turn aside, and see this great sight, why the bush is not burnt. [4] And when the LORD saw that he turned aside to see, God called unto him out of the midst of the bush, and said, Moses, Moses. And he said, Here *am* I. [5] And he said, Draw not nigh hither: put off thy shoes from off thy feet, for the place whereon thou standest *is* holy ground.

Put off thy shoes: to loosen (remove) one's shoes was a symbolic action of humility and reverence occurring elsewhere in scripture (cf. Josh. 5:15). It was also a custom within the laws of Levirate marriage (cf. Deut. 25:9; Ruth 4:7) and is still custom practiced by many Eastern religions. Here, for the first time in scripture, the idea of sacred space is introduced whereas only sacred time preceded (i.e. the Sabbath). The elements of spatial sanctity would be further established in the construction and erection of the Tabernacle of God, where many believe the priesthood approached barefoot as they administered the functions of the House of God.

⁶ Moreover he said, I *am* the God of thy father, the God of Abraham, the God of Isaac, and the God of Jacob. And Moses hid his face; for he was afraid to look upon God.

Hearkening back to God's remembrance of the covenant with Abraham, here God emphasizes to Moses the Patriarchal connection. Though **father** is used here in the singular, Acts 7:32 uses the plural *fathers*, holding to the threefold paternal structure in scripture. Upon hearing the identity of the voice, Moses hides his face, a sharp contrast to his later request to see the glory of God (cf. Ex 33:18).

⁷ And the LORD said, I have surely seen the affliction of my people which are in Egypt, and have heard their cry by reason of their taskmasters; for I know their sorrows; ⁸ And I am come down to deliver them out of the hand of the Egyptians, and to bring them up out of that land unto a good land and a large, unto a land flowing with milk and honey; unto the place of the Canaanites, and the Hittites, and the Amorites, and the Perizzites, and the Hivites, and the Jebusites. ⁹ Now therefore, behold,

the cry of the children of Israel is come unto me: and I have also seen the oppression wherewith the Egyptians oppress them. 10 Come now therefore, and I will send thee unto Pharaoh, that thou mayest bring forth my people the children of Israel out of Egypt.

I am come down: The idea of God coming down merely implies the divine decision to intervene in human affairs, as seen in the building of the Tower of Babel (cf. Gen. 11:5). This phrase, as are other anthropomorphic figures of speech, bring clarity to the operation of God within the world. Covenantal remembrance (see commentary on 2:24) brings about the decisive action of God, beginning first on the peripheral of Moses' life.

[11] **And Moses said unto God, Who** *am* **I, that I should go unto Pharaoh, and that I should bring forth the children of Israel out of Egypt?**

Who am I stands in stark contrast to the former, **I am the God of your father** (vs. 6). This will begin a narrative of divine revelation where God establishes His transcendent identity and the placement and empowerment Moses is meant to have within the said revealed identity.

[12] **And he said, Certainly I will be with thee; and this** *shall be* **a token unto thee, that I have sent thee: When thou hast brought forth the people out of Egypt, ye shall serve God upon this mountain.**

This shall be a token unto thee: the token (lit. *sign*) of God's promise to be with Moses is a little ambiguous. Contextually, the promise of *abiding presence* marked by the promise of **I will be with thee**, would seem to serve as the sign of God's visible appointment and commission (cf. Ex. 33:15-16). This holds to the authenticating aspect of the Spirit of God among individuals and people throughout scripture.

[13] And Moses said unto God, Behold, *when* I come unto the children of Israel, and shall say unto them, The God of your fathers hath sent me unto you; and they shall say to me, What is his name? what shall I say unto them?

Interestingly, Moses does not express that the God of our fathers hath sent me, but rather, the God of your fathers hath sent me. This may lend toward the idea that Moses, while having a general knowledge of the God of Israel, was not acquainted yet with the specifics of Jehovah. Therefore, **what shall I say unto them** when they ask me, **what is his name?** Indeed, the people would seek to verify the validity of the claim that their God had commissioned Moses to bring them out of Egypt.

[14] And God said unto Moses, I AM THAT I AM: and he said, Thus shalt thou say unto the children of Israel, I AM hath sent me unto you. [15] And God said moreover unto Moses, Thus shalt thou say unto the children of Israel, The LORD God of your fathers, the God of Abraham, the God of Isaac, and the God of Jacob, hath sent me unto you: this *is* my name for ever, and this *is* my memorial unto all generations.

I AM THAT I AM: The Hebrew expression, הָיָה אֲשֶׁר הֶיְהֶא (*Ehyeh-Asher-Ehyeh*), is not so much a name as it is an identity that establishes the underlying preeminence and sovereignty of God's name, YHWH (vs. 15). It is an expression pointing to the absolute, self-existent, eternal nature of God. Unlike the pluralistic gods of Egypt, the I AM was not created, shaped, or birthed into existence. In Isaiah 43:10, God declares that before or after Him no other God was formed. He is not a God among gods, rather, He is the *only true God* (cf. Jer. 10:10; Jn. 17:3).

This self-existent, eternal nature of God was declared by Jesus Christ as *the alpha and omega* that *was, is, and is to come* (Rev. 1:8). The same *I AM* that would save Israel from Egypt was the same *I AM*, in flesh, that would save the world from their sins (cf. II Cor. 5:19). Moses' commissioning authority was I AM (3:14b), earlier revealed to be a token (lit. sign or banner) to Moses (vs.11). This token of God's presence, the I AM, is elsewhere brought up by Moses as the only decisive difference between the nation of Israel and the other nations of the world (cf. Ex. 33:15).

The LORD God of thy fathers...this is my name: Moving from the broad, *I AM* expression, God declares His name as הָוֹהִי, (YHWH), narrowing down to a relationship-specific identity with the children of Israel that moved from the general understanding of the self-existent, eternal God to the personal God of Patriarchal promises.

16 Go, and gather the elders of Israel together, and say unto them, The LORD God of your fathers, the God of Abraham, of Isaac, and of Jacob, appeared unto me, saying, I have surely visited you, and *seen* that which is done to you in Egypt: **17** And I have said, I will bring you up out of the affliction of Egypt unto the land of the Canaanites, and the Hittites, and the Amorites, and the Perizzites, and the Hivites, and the Jebusites, unto a land flowing with milk and honey.

From bitter herbs to milk and honey, God intended to fulfil His promise to Abraham. The expression *milk and honey* served as a euphemism of the abundance and fruitfulness of the land God has promised the children of Israel (cf. Ezek. 20:6).

¹⁸ **And they shall hearken to thy voice: and thou shalt come, thou and the elders of Israel, unto the king of Egypt, and ye shall say unto him, The LORD God of the Hebrews hath met with us: and now let us go, we beseech thee, three days' journey into the wilderness, that we may sacrifice to the LORD our God. ¹⁹ And I am sure that the king of Egypt will not let you go, no, not by a mighty hand. ²⁰ And I will stretch out my hand, and smite Egypt with all my wonders which I will do in the midst thereof: and after that he will let you go. ²¹ And I will give this people favour in the sight of the Egyptians: and it shall come to pass, that, when ye go, ye shall not go empty:**

Moses is told from the outset that the request to leave **three days' journey** to sacrifice will not be granted by Pharaoh, not even by a **mighty hand** (lit. *force*). Nothing Moses would say or do would cause their release, therefore God would stretch forth His hand and strike Egypt with **wonders** אָלְפ (*pālā'*) meaning *something extraordinary*, implying that which *surpasses comprehension*. These wonders (ten plagues) would bring Pharaoh to a place of surrender and allow for the children of Israel to go free.

The words **ye shall not go empty** summons up similar language concerning the law regarding the inevitable freedom of Hebrew slaves (cf. Deut. 15:13-14). In this case, Israel had served the years required by Divine providence (cf. Gen. 15:13; Ex. 12:40-41). With this fulfilment of servitude, divine mandate had expressed Egypt's responsibility to reward Israel, perspective of their years of bondage, an action the Egyptians would do without compulsion.

[22] But every woman shall borrow of her neighbour, and of her that sojourneth in her house, jewels of silver, and jewels of gold, and raiment: and ye shall put *them* upon your sons, and upon your daughters; and ye shall spoil the Egyptians.

The Septuagint renders **borrow** as *ask*, which is supported by the Hebrew equivalent לִשְׁאַל (*sha'al*) found throughout scriptures. Certainly, with those either sympathetic or those altogether ready to rid themselves of the troublesome Hebrews, it would appear as though the Israelites had **spoiled** the Egyptians.

Notes

CHAPTER FOUR

¹ **And Moses answered and said, But, behold, they will not believe me, nor hearken unto my voice: for they will say, The LORD hath not appeared unto thee.**

Moses would respond to God's request with three protests. The first protest, the people will say **the LORD hath not appeared unto thee**, is met with the question **what is in thine hand?** Three signs would follow, also called **voices** (vs. 8) since these signs would *speak* to the claim of Moses that God (I AM THAT I AM) had sent him.

² **And the LORD said unto him, What is that in thine hand? And he said, A rod.** ³ **And he said, Cast it on the ground. And he cast it on the ground, and it became a serpent; and Moses fled from before it.** ⁴ **And the LORD said unto Moses, Put forth thine hand, and take it by the tail. And he put forth his hand, and caught it, and it became a rod in his hand:** ⁵ **That they may believe that the LORD God of their fathers, the God of Abraham, the God of Isaac, and the God of Jacob, hath appeared unto thee.**

The <u>first sign</u> involved the casting down of the rod that was in Moses' hand. When Moses cast it down it became a נָחָשׁ (nāhāsh), a general term for *serpent*. Grasping the serpent by the tail resulted in the serpent becoming a rod again.

⁶ And the LORD said furthermore unto him, Put now thine hand into thy bosom. And he put his hand into his bosom: and when he took it out, behold, his hand *was* leprous as snow. ⁷ And he said, Put thine hand into thy bosom again. And he put his hand into his bosom again; and plucked it out of his bosom, and, behold, it was turned again as his *other* flesh.

The second sign involved Moses putting his hand into his bosom (lit. chest) and upon taking it out, found it to be **leprous as snow**. Repeating the process, putting the leprous hand into his chest and then removing, would find his hand clean once again. Not only did God control the rod but God controlled the hand which wielded the rod.

⁸ And it shall come to pass, if they will not believe thee, neither hearken to the voice of the first sign, that they will believe the voice of the latter sign. ⁹ And it shall come to pass, if they will not believe also these two signs, neither hearken unto thy voice, that thou shalt take of the water of the river, and pour it upon the dry *land*: and the water which thou takest out of the river shall become blood upon the dry *land*.

Finally, if the voice of the first two signs were not enough to convince the people then a third sign would be enacted before the elders and children of Israel in Egypt. Moses was to take water from the Nile river and pour it upon dry ground. Similar to the first plague, though in reverse, the water poured upon dry ground would become blood.

[10] And Moses said unto the LORD, O my Lord, I *am* not eloquent, neither heretofore, nor since thou hast spoken unto thy servant: but I *am* slow of speech, and of a slow tongue. [11] And the LORD said unto him, Who hath made man's mouth? or who maketh the dumb, or deaf, or the seeing, or the blind? have not I the LORD? [12] Now therefore go, and I will be with thy mouth, and teach thee what thou shalt say.

Neither before nor since God had begun speaking to him did Moses feel that he was eloquent, (lit. a *man of words*). Going further, he complained that he was slow כָּבֵד. (*kābēd*) meaning ***heavy***, of speech and tongue. This does not mean with certainty that Moses had a speech impediment, though it is possible. More than likely, it points towards Moses' personal perception of his speaking abilities and his insecurity in being the one to proclaim God's word (cf. Jer. 1:4-9).

Defeating this objection, God poses a rhetorical question, **who hath made man's mouth?** The prior demonstrations of God's power over the rod and hand should have made it evidently clear that God can also control and empower the mouth. If God can open the mouth of a donkey (Num. 22:30), so then can God magnify the ability of man's articulation. New Testament scripture indicates this is exactly what happened, declaring Moses as a man *mighty in words* (Acts. 7:22).

[13] And he said, O my Lord, send, I pray thee, by the hand *of him whom* thou wilt send.

The Septuagint renders this as, *Elect another powerful person, whom thou might send,* revealing a begrudging obedience from Moses that implies a brazen unspoken, *"go find someone else"*. This response would cause God's anger to "burn" against Moses.

¹⁴ And the anger of the LORD was kindled against Moses, and he said, Is not Aaron the Levite thy brother? I know that he can speak well. And also, behold, he cometh forth to meet thee: and when he seeth thee, he will be glad in his heart.

Seeming to anticipate Moses' stubborn protests, God has already set into motion events that would silence any further protest. Mentioned for the first time in scripture, Moses' brother Aaron is said to be arriving to assist in God's plans. The identification of Aaron as **the Levite** is unique and scholars are divided as to its intention. More than likely, since the Levitical priesthood is yet to be established, it is meant as a wordplay, since Levi means *"to join"* (cf. Num. 28:2).

¹⁵ And thou shalt speak unto him, and put words in his mouth: and I will be with thy mouth, and with his mouth, and will teach you what ye shall do. ¹⁶ And he shall be thy spokesman unto the people: and he shall be, even he shall be to thee instead of a mouth, and thou shalt be to him instead of God.

It was not uncommon for kings to have intermediaries that served as the **mouth** (voice) of the king. Though not a king, Moses would join with Aaron and a unique (top-down) communicative relationship would be utilized. God would speak to Moses, Moses would speak to Aaron, and Aaron would speak to the people.

It needs to be noted that this was probably not the case as it related to communication with Pharaoh.

¹⁷ And thou shalt take this rod in thine hand, wherewith thou shalt do signs. ¹⁸ And Moses went and returned to Jethro his father in law, and said unto him, Let me go, I pray thee, and return unto my brethren which *are* **in Egypt, and see whether they be yet alive. And Jethro said to Moses, Go in peace.**

One cannot overlook the responsibility Moses had toward the flock of Jethro nor the obvious respect and deference Moses had for his father-in-law. However, Moses does not tell Jethro the true reason for his return to Egypt nor does he entirely tell the truth, since God had already revealed the status of his brethren.

¹⁹ And the LORD said unto Moses in Midian, Go, return into Egypt: for all the men are dead which sought thy life. ²⁰ And Moses took his wife and his sons, and set them upon an ass, and he returned to the land of Egypt: and Moses took the rod of God in his hand. ²¹ And the LORD said unto Moses, When thou goest to return into Egypt, see that thou do all those wonders before Pharaoh, which I have put in thine hand: but I will harden his heart, that he shall not let the people go. ²² And thou shalt say unto Pharaoh, Thus saith the LORD, Israel is my son, *even* **my firstborn: ²³ And I say unto thee, Let my son go, that he may serve me: and if thou refuse to let him go, behold, I will slay thy son,** *even* **thy firstborn.**

Here for the first time the children of Israel are called God's **firstborn** רְכֹּב (*bekôr*). The significance of this expression finds clarity in God's focus upon the firstborn of Egypt that culminates in the 10ᵗʰ plague. The war upon Egypt's firstborn is simple. The generation of Hebrews under the yoke of Egyptian bondage was **the generation of promised inheritance** (cf. Gen. 15: 13-16). Therefore, if Pharaoh refused to let God's inheritor go free then God would slay Pharaoh and all of Egypt's inheritor.

²⁴ And it came to pass by the way in the inn, that the LORD met him, and sought to kill him. ²⁵ Then Zipporah took a sharp stone, and cut off the foreskin of her son, and cast it at his feet, and said, Surely a bloody husband *art* thou to me. ²⁶ So he let him go: then she said, A bloody husband *thou art*, because of the circumcision.

Moses' sin is never explicitly stated nor is the means by which God sought to kill him. However, this brief narrative immediately follows the deliberate plan of God to free His *firstborn of inheritance*. Moses' obvious neglect to circumcise his child (most likely his firstborn son Gershom) is a gross oversight on Moses' part. A covenant of blood had been instituted between God and Abraham and the sign of the covenant had been ratified by circumcision (Gen. 17:9-14). Before Moses could ever bring the children of Israel into covenant promise he had to cease from being a covenant-breaker. It is interesting to note that under the leadership of Moses the nation of Israel did not circumcise their male infants in the wilderness, a practice that was changed under the leadership of Joshua (Josh. 5:2-8).

A bloody husband: חֲתַן־דָּמִים, (*hatan-damim*), literally, *bridegroom of blood*. The Hebrew verb נָגַע (*nāga*), used when Zipporah cast the foreskin at Moses' feet, is the same verb used for the application of blood to the lintel and doorposts of the Hebrew homes to avoid the judgment of God against the firstborn (cf. Ex. 12:22). However, just as blood averted the death of the firstborn in Egypt so now blood would avert the death of Moses' son.

²⁷ And the LORD said to Aaron, Go into the wilderness to meet Moses. And he went, and met him in the mount of God, and kissed him. ²⁸ And Moses told Aaron all the words of the LORD who had sent him, and all the signs which he had commanded him. ²⁹ And Moses and Aaron went and gathered together all the elders of the children of Israel: ³⁰ And Aaron spake all the words which the LORD had spoken unto Moses, and did the signs in the sight of the people. ³¹ And the people believed: and when they heard that the LORD had visited the children of Israel, and that he had looked upon their affliction, then they bowed their heads and worshipped.

It is unknown if all three signs were required before the children of Israel believed the words of Moses, as relayed by Aaron. However, the unique relationship of Moses and Aaron is displayed for the first time here. The response of the people is one of humility, that the Lord would look upon their affliction and seek to deliver them.

Notes

CHAPTER FIVE

Exodus 5:1-23 (KJV)
¹ And afterward Moses and Aaron went in, and told Pharaoh, Thus saith the LORD God of Israel, Let my people go, that they may hold a feast unto me in the wilderness.

It is unclear the intentions God had when he commanded Moses to request a three-day's journey into the wilderness to hold a feast. With the foreknowledge that Pharaoh would not yield to the demands of God (3:19) it seems mere lip service to request the excursion to hold a feast, a word that implies a ritual pilgrimage celebration.

² And Pharaoh said, Who *is* the LORD, that I should obey his voice to let Israel go? I know not the LORD, neither will I let Israel go.

The Egyptians were severe polytheists, paying tribute and service to a multiplicity of gods, but Pharaoh declares his ignorance of YHWH. One of the primary reasons that God would go through the lengthy process to follow was that, before Israel is released, His absolute and exclusive sovereignty would be known among those of Egypt (cf. 7:5; 14:18). This is an important feature of the plague narrative since God could have delivered Israel hastily. Instead, deliverance is submitted to a process that will gradually bring Egypt to their knees in submission lest anyone say that it was Pharaoh that allowed Israel to leave.

³ **And they said, The God of the Hebrews hath met with us: let us go, we pray thee, three days' journey into the desert, and sacrifice unto the LORD our God; lest he fall upon us with pestilence, or with the sword.**

Lest he fall upon us with pestilence, or with the sword: there has never been mention of God implying judgment by pestilence or sword if the Israelites failed to sacrifice in the desert. This addition to God's word may have been an attempt by Moses and Aaron to appeal to the polytheistic viewpoint of deity. That is, Pharaoh could understand the desire to appease a god, a practice common to polytheistic rituals.

⁴ **And the king of Egypt said unto them, Wherefore do ye, Moses and Aaron, let the people from their works? get you unto your burdens. ⁵ And Pharaoh said, Behold, the people of the land now** *are* **many, and ye make them rest from their burdens. ⁶ And Pharaoh commanded the same day the taskmasters of the people, and their officers, saying, ⁷ Ye shall no more give the people straw to make brick, as heretofore: let them go and gather straw for themselves. ⁸ And the tale of the bricks, which they did make heretofore, ye shall lay upon them; ye shall not diminish** *ought* **thereof: for they** *be* **idle; therefore they cry, saying, Let us go** *and* **sacrifice to our God. ⁹ Let there more work be laid upon the men, that they may labour therein; and let them not regard**

vain words. ¹⁰ And the taskmasters of the people went out, and their officers, and they spake to the people, saying, Thus saith Pharaoh, I will not give you straw. ¹¹ Go ye, get you straw where ye can find it: yet not ought of your work shall be diminished. ¹² So the people were scattered abroad throughout all the land of Egypt to gather stubble instead of straw.

Ye shall no more give the people straw to make brick: brick was made mixing clay and sand, adding straw to give it greater cohesion. After hearing the request of Moses for the slaves to take a three-day journey into the wilderness to feast and sacrifice unto their God, which would translate as a 6 or 7-day furlough, Pharaoh charges them with being idle (lit. lazy) and demands the same production as before the restriction. Such an action causes the Israelites to be **scattered abroad...to gather stubble instead of straw:** they were relegated to gather the dried-out chaff that remained in the fields after the harvesting had occurred.

¹³ And the taskmasters hasted *them*, saying, Fulfil your works, *your* daily tasks, as when there was straw. ¹⁴ And the officers of the children of Israel, which Pharaoh's taskmasters had set over them, were beaten, *and* demanded, Wherefore have ye not fulfilled your task in making brick both yesterday and to day, as heretofore? ¹⁵ Then the officers of the children of Israel came and cried unto Pharaoh, saying, Wherefore dealest thou thus with thy servants? ¹⁶ There is no straw given unto thy servants, and they say to us, Make brick: and, behold, thy servants *are* beaten; but the fault *is* in thine own people. ¹⁷ But he said, Ye *are* idle, *ye are* idle: therefore ye say, Let us go *and* do sacrifice

to the LORD. ¹⁸ Go therefore now, *and* work; for there shall no straw be given you, yet shall ye deliver the tale of bricks.

Ye are idle, ye are idle: double emphasis is articulated by Pharaoh as he denounces the Israelites as a *lazy, lazy* people. It is a backhanded slight on the part of Pharaoh, knowing that the children of Israel were anything but lazy. However, the point is clearly to oppose Moses' request and turn it upon the people in a way that causes them to regret their association and alignment with Moses and Aaron.

¹⁹ And the officers of the children of Israel did see *that* they *were* in evil *case*, after it was said, Ye shall not minish *ought* from your bricks of your daily task. ²⁰ And they met Moses and Aaron, who stood in the way, as they came forth from Pharaoh: ²¹ And they said unto them, The LORD look upon you, and judge; because ye have made our savour to be abhorred in the eyes of Pharaoh, and in the eyes of his servants, to put a sword in their hand to slay us. ²² And Moses returned unto the LORD, and said, Lord, wherefore hast thou so evil entreated this people? why *is* it *that* thou hast sent me? ²³ For since I came to Pharaoh to speak in thy name, he hath done evil to this people; neither hast thou delivered thy people at all.

Ye have made our savour to be abhorred: finding Moses and Aaron on the path, the officers lamented their current condition and exaggerating it to the point of declaring that Pharaoh and the Egyptians couldn't even stand the *smell* of the Hebrews, an interesting statement considering the Egyptian's aforementioned loathing of the Hebrews (1:12). Not understanding that these were merely the early contractions of deliverance, the Hebrew people would find themselves amid a carefully designed strategy that would eventually conclude with bloody lintels and dying firstborns.

Notes

CHAPTER SIX

¹ Then the LORD said unto Moses, Now shalt thou see what I will do to Pharaoh: for with a strong hand shall he let them go, and with a strong hand shall he drive them out of his land. ² And God spake unto Moses, and said unto him, I am the LORD:

The authoritative declaration, **I am the LORD**, was a common literary expression of ancient eastern kings (with their own names inserted) whenever a proclamation was given. Here there is a threefold repetition of this expression (vss. 2, 7, 8), holding to the formula of the proclamations of human kings.

³ And I appeared unto Abraham, unto Isaac, and unto Jacob, by *the name of* **God Almighty, but by my name JEHOVAH was I not known to them.**

By my name JEHOVAH was I not known to them: This does not imply that the name JEHOVAH has never been used until this point, since it indeed had been (cf. Gen. 2:4, 15:4, 7). The emphasis of this is upon the connotation of the name. The Patriarch's had known God within the scope of His sufficiency, as well as in fruitfulness and increase. On the other hand, the generation

Moses was commissioned to lead was the recipient of verbiage that indicated a unique relationship with God. God had called them His *firstborn son* based upon the implication that they would inherit both the genealogical and geographical promises given to the Patriarchs. The generation that Moses was commissioned to lead would know Jehovah in both the fulfilment and redemptive qualities the name signified. A great degree of personalization accompanies those who experientially realize the qualities and character that the name Jehovah signifies. This is expressed even more so, beginning and ending with the authoritative expression of **I am the Lord**, when the redemption, adoptive, and paternal characteristics of Jehovah are revealed through the seven **I will's** (vss. 6:6-8). The generation Moses had been called to were <u>children of possession</u> whereas the Patriarchs were the <u>fathers of promise</u>. As the firstborn conceived in the womb of Egypt, soon to be delivered through the waters of the Red Sea, and later adopted as sons at Sinai, they would experience the very qualities of JEHOVAH whom Abraham had lifted his hands and proclaiming as the possessor of the heavens and the earth (Gen. 14:22).

⁴ And I have also established my covenant with them, to give them the land of Canaan, the land of their pilgrimage, wherein they were strangers. ⁵ And I have also heard the groaning of the children of Israel, whom the Egyptians keep in bondage; and I have remembered my covenant. ⁶ Wherefore say unto the children of Israel, I *am* the LORD, and I will bring you out from under the burdens of the Egyptians, and I will rid you out of their bondage, and I will redeem you with a stretched out arm, and with great judgments:

I will redeem you with a stretched out arm: Scripture is heavy with the anthropomorphic expressions of God's intervening arm and hand. In the book of Isaiah, the rhetorical question is asked: *is my hand shortened at all, that it cannot redeem?* (Isa. 50:2a). A continual motif will be cast throughout the book of Exodus that contrasts the arm and hand of God against the hand and arm of Egypt. Pharaoh, *not by a mighty hand* (Ex. 3:19) will let the children of Israel go. Gods outstretched, never-shortened arm and hand will prevail against the powers of Egypt.

⁷ And I will take you to me for a people, and I will be to you a God: and ye shall know that I *am* the LORD your God, which bringeth you out from under the burdens of the Egyptians. ⁸ And I will bring you in unto the land, concerning the which I did swear to give it to Abraham, to Isaac, and to Jacob; and I will give it you for an heritage: I *am* the LORD.

Ye shall now that I am the LORD your God: not only would God initiate great judgments upon Egypt that would inform them of His sovereignty but God would also use the events of redemption to establish His paternal relationship with Israel; a relationship unlike any of the pagan gods or Egypt's religious system.

⁹ And Moses spake so unto the children of Israel: but they hearkened not unto Moses for anguish of spirit, and for cruel bondage. ¹⁰ And the LORD spake unto Moses, saying, ¹¹ Go in, speak unto Pharaoh king of Egypt, that he let the children of Israel go out of his land. ¹² And Moses spake before the LORD, saying, Behold, the children of Israel have not hearkened unto me; how then shall Pharaoh hear me, who am of uncircumcised lips? ¹³

And the LORD spake unto Moses and unto Aaron, and gave them a charge unto the children of Israel, and unto Pharaoh king of Egypt, to bring the children of Israel out of the land of Egypt.

How then shall Pharaoh hear me, who *am* **of uncircumcised lips:** this first half (*how shall Pharaoh hear me*) is not a reiteration of Moses' former doubts of himself, but rather, a statement that expresses a very real predicament. In other words, *if the very people whom you seek to deliver will not listen to me, how then should I expect Pharaoh, one that is not of your people, to hear me?* Reverting once again to the aforementioned principle of his speech being an issue, Moses claims to be of **uncircumcised lips** only this time he is expressing, not a slowness or heaviness of speech, but his not being prepared or ready to speak. The imagery of circumcision is here meant to apply to the lips and the mouth of speech.

[14] These *be* **the heads of their fathers' houses: The sons of Reuben the firstborn of Israel; Hanoch, and Pallu, Hezron, and Carmi: these** *be* **the families of Reuben. [15] And the sons of Simeon; Jemuel, and Jamin, and Ohad, and Jachin, and Zohar, and Shaul the son of a Canaanitish woman: these** *are* **the families of Simeon. [16] And these** *are* **the names of the sons of Levi according to their generations; Gershon, and Kohath, and Merari: and the years of the life of Levi were an hundred thirty and seven years. [17] The sons of Gershon; Libni, and Shimi, according to their families. [18] And the sons of Kohath; Amram, and Izhar, and Hebron, and Uzziel: and the years of the life of Kohath** *were* **an hundred thirty and three years. [19] And the sons of Merari; Mahali and Mushi: these** *are* **the families of Levi according to their generations.**

²⁰ And Amram took him Jochebed his father's sister to wife; and she bare him Aaron and Moses: and the years of the life of Amram *were* an hundred and thirty and seven years. ²¹ And the sons of Izhar; Korah, and Nepheg, and Zichri. ²² And the sons of Uzziel; Mishael, and Elzaphan, and Zithri. ²³ And Aaron took him Elisheba, daughter of Amminadab, sister of Naashon, to wife; and she bare him Nadab, and Abihu, Eleazar, and Ithamar. ²⁴ And the sons of Korah; Assir, and Elkanah, and Abiasaph: these *are* the families of the Korhites. ²⁵ And Eleazar Aaron's son took him *one* of the daughters of Putiel to wife; and she bare him Phinehas: these *are* the heads of the fathers of the Levites according to their families. ²⁶ These *are* that Aaron and Moses, to whom the LORD said, Bring out the children of Israel from the land of Egypt according to their armies. ²⁷ These *are* they which spake to Pharaoh king of Egypt, to bring out the children of Israel from Egypt: these are that Moses and Aaron.

The lengthy genealogical insertion (**14-26**) seems out of place amid the Exodus narrative. However, the primary aim of the genealogy is to highlight the pedigree of Moses and Aaron (26) and to highlight the pedigree of the Levitical family (25).

²⁸ And it came to pass on the day *when* the LORD spake unto Moses in the land of Egypt, ²⁹ That the LORD spake unto Moses, saying, I *am* the LORD: speak thou unto Pharaoh king of Egypt all that I say unto thee. ³⁰ And Moses said before the LORD, Behold, I *am* of uncircumcised lips, and how shall Pharaoh hearken unto me?

Notes

CHAPTER SEVEN

¹ And the LORD said unto Moses, See, I have made thee a god to Pharaoh: and Aaron thy brother shall be thy prophet.

I have made thee a God to Pharaoh: Recognized as a god among gods, Pharaoh would have interpreted the unique relationship with Moses and Aaron from the platform of a polytheistic viewpoint. This is further established that, in the eyes of Pharaoh, Aaron would appear as Moses' prophet, declaring the words of Moses.

² Thou shalt speak all that I command thee: and Aaron thy brother shall speak unto Pharaoh, that he send the children of Israel out of his land. ³ And I will harden Pharaoh's heart, and multiply my signs and my wonders in the land of Egypt. ⁴ But Pharaoh shall not hearken unto you, that I may lay my hand upon Egypt, and bring forth mine armies, *and* my people the children of Israel, out of the land of Egypt by great judgments. ⁵ And the Egyptians shall know that I *am* the LORD, when I stretch forth mine hand upon Egypt, and bring out the children of Israel from among them. ⁶ And Moses and Aaron did as the LORD commanded them, so did they.

Here the outline of God's plan gives greater understanding as to why He would go through the lengthy process of delivering His people. Surely, had God wanted to bring the children of Israel out of Egypt it could have been swift and immediate. However, the statement, **the Egyptians shall know that I am the LORD** reveals the fullness of Gods intentions. There would be no misunderstanding as to the nature of Israel's deliverance. None would place their freedom upon the generosity of Pharaoh, but rather, all would know that **I am the LORD.**

⁷ And Moses *was* **fourscore years old, and Aaron fourscore and three years old, when they spake unto Pharaoh. ⁸ And the LORD spake unto Moses and unto Aaron, saying, ⁹ When Pharaoh shall speak unto you, saying, Shew a miracle for you: then thou shalt say unto Aaron, Take thy rod, and cast** *it* **before Pharaoh,** *and* **it shall become a serpent. ¹⁰ And Moses and Aaron went in unto Pharaoh, and they did so as the LORD had commanded: and Aaron cast down his rod before Pharaoh, and before his servants, and it became a serpent. ¹¹ Then Pharaoh also called the wise men and the sorcerers: now the magicians of Egypt, they also did in like manner with their enchantments. ¹² For they cast down every man his rod, and they became serpents: but Aaron's rod swallowed up their rods.**

Take thy rod...it shall become a serpent: Aaron's rod is clearly distinguished from Moses' rod and this distinction will continue to play an important role throughout the plague narrative (cf. 7:19; 8:5; 8:16). In this case, unlike the throwing down of Moses' rod at the burning bush which became a serpent שָׁחָנ (*nāhāsh*), Aaron's rod would become a תַּנִּין, (*tannin*), which marks a signalled difference. The Hebrew word וְתַנִּין (*tannin*), especially in context of Egypt, means <u>crocodile</u>. The metaphor is used of Pharaoh, likened to a great dragon וְתַנִּין, (*tannin*) in the midst of the Nile River (Ezek. 29:3), even a dragon וְתַנִּין (*tannin*), that muddies and pollutes the waters of the river (Ezek. 32:2). This is an important point as it relates to Aaron's rod being cast down before the eyes of Pharaoh and the subsequent action of the two magicians, Jannes and Jambres (II Tim. 3:8), casting down their rods which also became וְתַנִּין (*tannin*). The incident of Aaron's crocodile devouring the crocodiles of the magicians would not be lost on Pharaoh and those present. The crocodiles, deeply feared and revered by the Egyptians, were considered to be ruled by the crocodile god, Sobek, also believed to have been the creator of the Nile River. Often depicted as a man with a crocodile head, Sobek was an important symbol of Pharaoh's power. When **Aaron's rod swallowed up their rods** it was as though God was declaring that Pharaoh and Egypt's Gods were nothing more than a rod in God's hand used to accomplish His divine purpose (cf. Ezek. 29:6).

13 And he hardened Pharaoh's heart, that he hearkened not unto them; as the LORD had said. 14 And the LORD said unto Moses, Pharaoh's heart is hardened, he refuseth to let the people go.

Pharaoh's heart is hardened: The hardening of Pharaoh's heart will find an interplay between two Hebrew words, חָזַק (*hāzaq*) meaning "*strengthened*" and כָּבֵד (*kābēd*) meaning "*heavy*". The vacillation between the two words reveals a unique pattern; the former revealing a strengthening of Pharaoh's resolve to stay the course and the latter, the heaviness of a stony heart that refused to bend in belief and submission.

¹⁵ Get thee unto Pharaoh in the morning; lo, he goeth out unto the water; and thou shalt stand by the river's brink against he come; and the rod which was turned to a serpent shalt thou take in thine hand.

The rod which was turned to a serpent: in contrast to Aaron's rod that had turned into a crocodile, God wanted Moses to use the rod that had become a serpent נָחָשׁ (*nāhāsh*), indicating the rod of Moses. With this rod, Moses was to smite (lit. *strike*) the Nile River and the waters of the river would be turned to blood.

¹⁶ And thou shalt say unto him, The LORD God of the Hebrews hath sent me unto thee, saying, Let my people go, that they may serve me in the wilderness: and, behold, hitherto thou wouldest not hear. ¹⁷ Thus saith the LORD, In this thou shalt know that I *am* the LORD: behold, I will smite with the rod that *is* in mine hand upon the waters which *are* in the river, and they shall be turned to blood. ¹⁸ And the fish that is in the river shall die, and the river shall stink; and the Egyptians shall lothe to drink of the water of the river.

Here begins the plague narrative which will follow a specific pattern. There are three cycles specific cycles which are as follows:

First Cycle	Second Cycle	Third Cycle
Blood	Swarm of Flies	Hail
Frogs	Pestilence	Locusts
Gnats	Boils	Darkness

It should be noted that, in each cycle, the first two plagues were initiated with a warning whereas the third plague of each cycle occurs without a warning. This systematic approach to the plagues reveals the design and intention of God and a plan that far exceeds judgment alone. In poet prose Psalm 78:43-51 and 105:27-36 are dedicated to the unfolding narrative of the plagues.

[19] And the LORD spake unto Moses, Say unto Aaron, Take thy rod, and stretch out thine hand upon the waters of Egypt, upon their streams, upon their rivers, and upon their ponds, and upon all their pools of water, that they may become blood; and *that* there may be blood throughout all the land of Egypt, both in *vessels of* wood, and in *vessels of* stone.

Aaron, take thy rod: Moses rod, having struck the Nile, has accomplished its purpose of directly affecting the river. Now, Aaron's rod is to once again be employed. By stretching his rod into the air, all over water exposed to the air would turn to blood, reflecting the condition of its source.

[20] And Moses and Aaron did so, as the LORD commanded; and he lifted up the rod, and smote the waters that were in the river, in the sight of Pharaoh, and in the sight of his servants; and all the waters that *were* in the river were turned to blood. [21] And the fish that *was* in the river died; and the river stank, and the Egyptians could not drink of the water of the river; and there was blood throughout all the land of Egypt. [22] And the magicians of Egypt did so with their enchantments: and Pharaoh's heart was hardened, neither did he hearken unto them; as the LORD had said.

The magicians of Egypt did so: it is unknown what source of water was available for the magicians of Egypt to employ their arts, though that they would have exacerbated the situation by divining the remaining good water into undrinkable, loathsome water.

[23] And Pharaoh turned and went into his house, neither did he set his heart to this also. [24] And all the Egyptians digged round about the river for water to drink; for they could not drink of the water of the river. [25] And seven days were fulfilled, after that the LORD had smitten the river.

Notes

CHAPTER EIGHT

¹ And the LORD spake unto Moses, Go unto Pharaoh, and say unto him, Thus saith the LORD, Let my people go, that they may serve me. ² And if thou refuse to let *them* go, behold, I will smite all thy borders with frogs: ³ And the river shall bring forth frogs abundantly, which shall go up and come into thine house, and into thy bedchamber, and upon thy bed, and into the house of thy servants, and upon thy people, and into thine ovens, and into thy kneadingtroughs: ⁴ And the frogs shall come up both on thee, and upon thy people, and upon all thy servants.

I will smite all thy borders with frogs: Egypt's deep veneration of the fertility goddess Heqt, a woman depicted with the head of a frog, would have made it impermissible for the Egyptians to kill the frogs. Because of this, what had served as an object of deity became a terrible pestilence to them.

⁵ And the LORD spake unto Moses, Say unto Aaron, Stretch forth thine hand with thy rod over the streams, over the rivers, and over the ponds, and cause frogs to come up upon the land of Egypt. ⁶ And Aaron stretched out his hand over the waters of Egypt; and the frogs came

up, and covered the land of Egypt. ⁷ And the magicians did so with their enchantments, and brought up frogs upon the land of Egypt. ⁸ Then Pharaoh called for Moses and Aaron, and said, Intreat the LORD, that he may take away the frogs from me, and from my people; and I will let the people go, that they may do sacrifice unto the LORD.

Intreat the LORD: already into the second plague, Pharaoh recognizes Yahweh, whom he prior declared ignorance. The underlying failure of the magicians to do away with the frogs, though they succeeded in bring frogs in, is revealed in Pharaoh's request to Moses.

⁹ And Moses said unto Pharaoh, Glory over me: when shall I intreat for thee, and for thy servants, and for thy people, to destroy the frogs from thee and thy houses, *that* they may remain in the river only?

Glory over me: is a unique phrase in the Hebrew. The Septuagint reads as, *appoint unto me*, but the most probable understanding of the phrase is that of *testing*. Pharaoh, one accustomed to a world of superstition and magic, would have felt a semblance of control so that he could challenge the veracity of the wonders brought forth by Moses' God by setting a fixed time for Moses' God to accomplish the cessation. The response by Pharaoh in the following verse, "**tomorrow**", מָחָר (*māhār*), signifying a *future time* (cf. Deut. 6:20, Josh. 4:6, 21), reinforces this view.

¹⁰ And he said, To morrow. And he said, *Be it* according to thy word: that thou mayest know that *there is* none like unto the LORD our God. ¹¹ And the frogs shall depart from thee, and from thy houses, and from thy servants, and from thy people; they shall remain in the river only.

The seemingly irrational request from Pharaoh that the frogs cease on the morrow finds its genius in the fact that Pharaoh, a polytheistic worshipper, has no problem accepting the veracity of a powerful god among gods. However, though a polytheistic worshipper can relate to the idea of gods being powerful, they cannot relate to a deity of whose power is played out in specific and exact timing. Their arcane arts may have articulated *estimated timing* based upon the various lunar and solar cycles of the heavens, but they could never comprehend a deity with the ability to operate under *exact* and *specific precision of timing*. As the plague narrative unfolds, this idea of precision continues to play an underlying theme (cf. Ex. 8:22; 9:4, 5, 18, 26; 10:4; 11:4). The God of Israel is a God, not only of power, but of exact precision.

[12] **And Moses and Aaron went out from Pharaoh: and Moses cried unto the LORD because of the frogs which he had brought against Pharaoh.** [13] **And the LORD did according to the word of Moses; and the frogs died out of the houses, out of the villages, and out of the fields.** [14] **And they gathered them together upon heaps: and the land stank.** [15] **But when Pharaoh saw that there was respite, he hardened his heart, and hearkened not unto them; as the LORD had said.**

[16] **And the LORD said unto Moses, Say unto Aaron, Stretch out thy rod, and smite the dust of the land, that it may become lice throughout all the land of Egypt.** [17] **And they did so; for Aaron stretched out his hand with his rod, and smote the dust of the earth, and it became lice in man, and in beast; all the dust of the land became lice throughout all the land of Egypt.** [18] **And the magicians did so with their enchantments to bring forth lice, but**

they could not: so there were lice upon man, and upon beast. [19] Then the magicians said unto Pharaoh, This is the finger of God: and Pharaoh's heart was hardened, and he hearkened not unto them; as the LORD had said.

The third plague, as well as the sixth and the ninth, come without warning to Pharaoh. Aaron is commanded to stretch forth his rod and smite the **dust of the land**, resulting in the dust becoming lice כִּנִּים (*kinnim*), something miniscule (gnat-like) with the ability to sting.

The magicians said…this is the finger of god: they do not say the finger of Yahweh, but instead use the general term for god, ***Elohim***. By doing this, they acknowledge that this miracle goes beyond Moses and Aaron and must be derived from some divine, unexplained assistance.

Pharaoh's heart was hardened: that is to say, his resolve was strengthened קָזַח (*ḥāzaq*), and he continued on his obstinate and stubborn course.

[20] And the LORD said unto Moses, Rise up early in the morning, and stand before Pharaoh; lo, he cometh forth to the water; and say unto him, Thus saith the LORD, Let my people go, that they may serve me. [21] Else, if thou wilt not let my people go, behold, I will send swarms *of flies* upon thee, and upon thy servants, and upon thy people, and into thy houses: and the houses of the Egyptians shall be full of swarms *of flies*, and also the ground whereon they *are*.

I will send swarms of flies upon thee: initiating the second cycle of plagues, God warns of a swarm, בָּעָרֹב

(ārōb), a Hebrew word used exclusively to identify the pestilence of the fourth plague found in this scripture (cf. Ps. 78:45; 105:31). Though it reads as **flies**, the most likely understanding is that of a *diverse mixture of harmful insects.*

²² And I will sever in that day the land of Goshen, in which my people dwell, that no swarms *of flies* shall be there; to the end thou mayest know that I *am* the LORD in the midst of the earth. ²³ And I will put a division between my people and thy people: to morrow shall this sign be.

I will sever in that day the land of Goshen: Not only was God able to control the specifics of timing, as shown in the plague of frogs, but he was also able to control the specifics of a plagues' reach within a geographical location. This would further establish Yahweh's sovereignty in the eyes of Pharaoh.

I will put a division: Most English translations follow the Septuagint's rendering of the word for division (Gk. *diastole*), meaning *distinction or difference*. However, the Hebrew, פְּדֻת (*pedût*), means **ransom or redemption** thus rendering the division between the Egyptians and Israelites as **redemption**. This idea of God setting redemption has interplay with the severing of the land of Goshen, where God clearly redeems with an outstretched hand (cf. Ex. 6:6), invoking the idea of God being able to protect within the very land He inflicts.

²⁴ And the LORD did so; and there came a grievous swarm *of flies* into the house of Pharaoh, and *into* his servants' houses, and into all the land of Egypt: the land was corrupted by reason of the swarm *of flies.* ²⁵ And

Pharaoh called for Moses and for Aaron, and said, Go ye, sacrifice to your God in the land.

Sacrifice to your God in the land: this is not to be viewed as a capitulation on the part of Pharaoh, for he merely implies that he is now willing to allow the Israelites to sacrifice, but only within the land of Egypt.

²⁶ And Moses said, It is not meet so to do; for we shall sacrifice the abomination of the Egyptians to the LORD our God: lo, shall we sacrifice the abomination of the Egyptians before their eyes, and will they not stone us?

Shall we sacrifice the abomination of the Egyptians before their eyes: this does not imply that the act of sacrificing was an abomination, though it would have been viewed as detestable in the eyes of the Egyptians. With alarming boldness, Moses refers to the sacred Egyptian bull-god Apis as an abomination (see II Kings 23:13, and the *abomination of the Zidonians*). Indeed, the idolatry and veneration of the beast-god Apis was an abomination in the eyes of God.

²⁷ We will go three days' journey into the wilderness, and sacrifice to the LORD our God, as he shall command us. ²⁸ And Pharaoh said, I will let you go, that ye may sacrifice to the LORD your God in the wilderness; only ye shall not go very far away: intreat for me.

Ye shall not go very far away: this is the first true form of Pharaoh's acquiescence to the request of Moses for Israel to sacrifice in the wilderness. However, Pharaoh refuses to relinquish control and specifies a limitation of distance that would nullify a three-day's journey.

²⁹ And Moses said, Behold, I go out from thee, and I will intreat the LORD that the swarms *of flies* may depart from Pharaoh, from his servants, and from his people, to morrow: but let not Pharaoh deal deceitfully any more in not letting the people go to sacrifice to the LORD. ³⁰ And Moses went out from Pharaoh, and intreated the LORD. ³¹ And the LORD did according to the word of Moses; and he removed the swarms *of flies* from Pharaoh, from his servants, and from his people; there remained not one. ³² And Pharaoh hardened his heart at this time also, neither would he let the people go.

Notes

CHAPTER NINE

¹ Then the LORD said unto Moses, Go in unto Pharaoh, and tell him, Thus saith the LORD God of the Hebrews, Let my people go, that they may serve me. ² For if thou refuse to let *them* go, and wilt hold them still, ³ Behold, the hand of the LORD is upon thy cattle which is in the field, upon the horses, upon the asses, upon the camels, upon the oxen, and upon the sheep: *there shall be* a very grievous murrain.

There shall be a very grievous murrain: The second plague of the second cycle, a very grievous murrain (lit. *exceeding heavy pestilence*), comes with the warning that the hand of God, as opposed to the *finger of God*, will be upon the livestock and beasts of burden of Egypt.

⁴ And the LORD shall sever between the cattle of Israel and the cattle of Egypt: and there shall nothing die of all *that is* the children's of Israel. ⁵ And the LORD appointed a set time, saying, To morrow the LORD shall do this thing in the land. ⁶ And the LORD did that thing on the morrow, and all the cattle of Egypt died: but of the cattle of the children of Israel died not one. ⁷ And Pharaoh sent, and, behold, there was not one of the

cattle of the Israelites dead. And the heart of Pharaoh was hardened, and he did not let the people go.

The LORD appointed a set time: once again, the precision of time plays an integral part in God's appointment of plagues. **On the morrow,** Pharaoh is seen showing little concern over the loss of his cattle, but instead, desires to know if not one of the cattle of Israel had perished. Surely, the great precision of God to isolate (**sever**) the cattle of Goshen from those of Egypt is staggering to the mindset of Pharaoh's religious ideology.

⁸ **And the LORD said unto Moses and unto Aaron, Take to you handfuls of ashes of the furnace, and let Moses sprinkle it toward the heaven in the sight of Pharaoh.** ⁹ **And it shall become small dust in all the land of Egypt, and shall be a boil breaking forth *with* blains upon man, and upon beast, throughout all the land of Egypt.**

Let Moses sprinkle it: this is the first time since the striking of the Nile River that Moses is directly involved in the causation of a plague, beyond commanding Aaron's actions. This marked change will set a pattern in the plagues to follow, for Aaron will not be called upon again to stretch forth his rod. Instead, each following plague will directly involve Moses as the intermediary to accomplish God's signs.

Boil breaking forth with blains: later scripture would point backwards to the knowledge of this plague, referring to it as the *botch of Egypt* (Deut. 28:27). The nature of the disease was marked by burning, inflamed sores that resulted in ruptured blisters. Similar suffering is found in the life of Job, whose only relief came from scraping the inflicted areas with a potsherd (Job 2:7).

[10] **And they took ashes of the furnace, and stood before Pharaoh; and Moses sprinkled it up toward heaven; and it became a boil breaking forth *with* blains upon man, and upon beast.** [11] **And the magicians could not stand before Moses because of the boils; for the boil was upon the magicians, and upon all the Egyptians.** [12] **And the LORD hardened the heart of Pharaoh, and he hearkened not unto them; as the LORD had spoken unto Moses.**

Ashes of the furnace: though the drying of bricks was commonly done under the power of the sun, there is evidence to indicate that brick kilns were in existence at the time of these events. In what seems poetic justice, the remnant of soot from the fashioning of bricks produced by forced, rigorous labor would be so severe that even the magicians were unable to appear due to the severity of the plague.

[13] **And the LORD said unto Moses, Rise up early in the morning, and stand before Pharaoh, and say unto him, Thus saith the LORD God of the Hebrews, Let my people go, that they may serve me.** [14] **For I will at this time send all my plagues upon thine heart, and upon thy servants, and upon thy people; that thou mayest know that *there* is none like me in all the earth.**

I will at this time send all my plagues upon thine heart...servants...people: At this time, that is to say, beginning with the final cycle of plagues which will lead to the death of the firstborn, God will strike directly at the very heart of the Egyptians. The increasing severity of these last three plagues would strike a devastating blow to the heart of their agricultural and economic systems, culminating in the devastation of darkness that crippled their movements, prayers, and daily oblations.

[15] For now I will stretch out my hand, that I may smite thee and thy people with pestilence; and thou shalt be cut off from the earth. 16 And in very deed for this *cause* have I raised thee up, for to shew *in* thee my power; and that my name may be declared throughout all the earth. [17] As yet exaltest thou thyself against my people, that thou wilt not let them go? [18] Behold, to morrow about this time I will cause it to rain a very grievous hail, such as hath not been in Egypt since the foundation thereof even until now.

For this cause have I raise thee up: literally, *for this cause have I kept thee alive*. God is revealing that, at any moment, he could have destroyed Pharaoh and Egypt. However, merely delivering Israel and destroying the Egyptians was not enough. God would be declared throughout all the earth, beginning with Pharaoh and the Egyptians first. (cf. Josh. 2:10; 9:9).

Behold, tomorrow, setting a fixed time lest anyone think it happenstance, God will **cause it to rain a very grievous hail**. Hail, though rare in Egypt, was not unknown to its inhabitants. However, this hail would be so catastrophic and devastating that it would be unlike anything the nation had ever known.

[19] Send therefore now, *and* gather thy cattle, and all that thou hast in the field; *for upon* every man and beast which shall be found in the field, and shall not be brought home, the hail shall come down upon them, and they shall die. [20] He that feared the word of the LORD

among the servants of Pharaoh made his servants and his cattle flee into the houses: ²¹ And he that regarded not the word of the LORD left his servants and his cattle in the field.

Send therefore now...gather thy cattle: with the promise of severe judgment comes a provision to escape the judgment. All Pharaoh had to do was to command that all cattle and servants be gathered into covered shelter. Instead, though some **feared the word of the LORD**, many paid no attention and left their servants and cattle in the field.

²² And the LORD said unto Moses, Stretch forth thine hand toward heaven, that there may be hail in all the land of Egypt, upon man, and upon beast, and upon every herb of the field, throughout the land of Egypt. ²³ And Moses stretched forth his rod toward heaven: and the LORD sent thunder and hail, and the fire ran along upon the ground; and the LORD rained hail upon the land of Egypt.

Moses stretched forth his rod: the first of many incidents in which Moses will be observed lifting his rod, which prior to this, had been an action of Aaron.

²⁴ So there was hail, and fire mingled with the hail, very grievous, such as there was none like it in all the land of Egypt since it became a nation. ²⁵ And the hail smote throughout all the land of Egypt all that *was* in the field, both man and beast; and the hail smote every herb of the field, and brake every tree of the field. ²⁶ Only in the land of Goshen, where the children of Israel *were*, was there no hail.

There was hail, and fire mingled with the hail: the scene being described is one of a cataclysmic thunderstorm that involved thunder, severe lighting, and monumental hail (cf. Ps. 18:13). It must have seemed as though all *the storehouses of hail* (Job 33:22) were being rained down on Egypt.

Only in the land of Goshen...no hail: once again, the precision of Israel's God to target a specific geographical location while excluding another is devastating to the Egyptians perception of deity. Not only would Yahweh claim the earth as His, but He would demonstrate His sovereignty over the very heavens above.

[27] And Pharaoh sent, and called for Moses and Aaron, and said unto them, I have sinned this time: the LORD is righteous, and I and my people *are* **wicked. [28] Intreat the LORD (for it is enough) that there be no** *more* **mighty thunderings and hail; and I will let you go, and ye shall stay no longer.**

I have sinned this time: it is unlikely that the verbiage being used by Pharaoh is one which translates into a contrast between sinfulness and righteousness. Instead, he uses the words within a legal context of right and wrong. He acknowledges that he is the guilty party, **this time**, and that YHWH is just and right. Though Pharaoh merely accepts error on his part on this particular event, it defies the supposed perception that Pharaoh was infallible and a god among gods.

[29] And Moses said unto him, As soon as I am gone out of the city, I will spread abroad my hands unto the LORD; *and* **the thunder shall cease, neither shall there be any more hail; that thou mayest know how that the earth** *is* the LORD'S. ³⁰ But as for thee and thy servants, I know that ye will not yet fear the LORD God. ³¹ And the flax and the barley *was* smitten: for the barley was in the ear, and the flax *was* bolled. ³² But the wheat and the rie were not smitten: for they *were* not grown up.

The wheat and the rie were not smitten: this small portion of text may seem extraneous but it merely indicates the desperate state of affairs that Egypt was finding itself in. The plagues were devastating the economy of Egypt and the only remaining agricultural sustenance to be found was in the early shoots of wheat and rye. God was attacking every facet of their economy.

³³ And Moses went out of the city from Pharaoh, and spread abroad his hands unto the LORD: and the thunders and hail ceased, and the rain was not poured upon the earth. ³⁴ And when Pharaoh saw that the rain and the hail and the thunders were ceased, he sinned yet more, and hardened his heart, he and his servants. ³⁵ And the heart of Pharaoh was hardened, neither would he let the children of Israel go; as the LORD had spoken by Moses.

He sinned yet more: that is to say, he **continued** to sin. After his declaration of **I have sinned** (27) the fear dissipates due to the cessation of the storm and he hardened דָּבֵכ (*kābēd*), made *heavy* his heart through purposeful resistance and stubbornness and the heart of Pharaoh was hardened (v.35) קָזָח (*hāzaq*), **strengthened** to stay the course and resolved to refuse Moses.

Notes

CHAPTER TEN

¹ And the LORD said unto Moses, Go in unto Pharaoh: for I have hardened his heart, and the heart of his servants, that I might shew these my signs before him: ² And that thou mayest tell in the ears of thy son, and of thy son's son, what things I have wrought in Egypt, and my signs which I have done among them; that ye may know how that I *am* the LORD.

Once again, God reiterates the purpose of the many signs and plagues in Egypt. In this case, the emphasis of knowing is placed upon the children of Israel. These events would serve to give the Israelites a testimony that they ma**yest tell in the ears of thy sons** and grandchildren the things God has **wrought in Egypt**.

³ And Moses and Aaron came in unto Pharaoh, and said unto him, Thus saith the LORD God of the Hebrews, How long wilt thou refuse to humble thyself before me? let my people go, that they may serve me. ⁴ Else, if thou refuse to let my people go, behold, to morrow will I bring the locusts into thy coast: ⁵ And they shall cover the face of the earth, that one cannot be able to see the earth: and they shall eat the residue of that which is escaped, which remaineth unto you from the hail, and shall eat every

tree which groweth for you out of the field: ⁶ And they shall fill thy houses, and the houses of all thy servants, and the houses of all the Egyptians; which neither thy fathers, nor thy fathers' fathers have seen, since the day that they were upon the earth unto this day. And he turned himself, and went out from Pharaoh.

I bring the locusts: The eighth plague of locusts הָאַרְבֶּה (*'arbeh*) would prove a devastating blow to the economy of Egypt. After the destruction of the seventh plague, the only crops remaining intact were the wheat and rye (9:32), along with some fruited trees. The plague of locusts, promised to be so great in number as to **cover the face** (lit. *eye*) **of the earth** (specifically Egypt), would **eat the residue of that which is escaped** the preceding plagues. An apt analogy of the devouring nature of this plague can be found in the progression of the locust, prophesied by Joel (cf. Joel 1:4).

⁷ **And Pharaoh's servants said unto him, How long shall this man be a snare unto us? let the men go, that they may serve the LORD their God: knowest thou not yet that Egypt is destroyed?**

Let the men go, that they may serve the Lord their God: recognizing the ruin that would completely devastate the economy of Egypt, Pharaohs advisors' council him to **let the men go for Egypt is destroyed.**

⁸ **And Moses and Aaron were brought again unto Pharaoh: and he said unto them, Go, serve the LORD your God:** *but* **who** *are* **they that shall go?** ⁹ **And Moses said, We will go with our young and with our old, with our sons and with our daughters, with our flocks and with our herds will we go; for we** *must hold* **a feast unto**

the LORD. ¹⁰ And he said unto them, Let the LORD be so with you, as I will let you go, and your little ones: look to it; for evil is before you. ¹¹ Not so: go now ye *that are* men, and serve the LORD; for that ye did desire. And they were driven out from Pharaoh's presence.

This is the first and last time that Pharaoh will be seen attempting to divert an impending plague. However, once again Pharaoh is unwilling to relinquish total control and poses the question to Moses: **who are they that shall go?** Upon Moses informing Pharaoh of the intention of the entirety of Israel, and their livestock as well, Pharaoh implements the advice of his counselors (7) declaring, **not so: go now ye that are men.**

And they were driven out: English translations lack the force of this verse for, quite literally, Moses and Aaron were forcibly cast out from the presence of Pharaoh.

¹² **And the LORD said unto Moses, Stretch out thine hand over the land of Egypt for the locusts, that they may come up upon the land of Egypt, and eat every herb of the land, *even* all that the hail hath left. ¹³ And Moses stretched forth his rod over the land of Egypt, and the LORD brought an east wind upon the land all that day, and all *that* night; *and* when it was morning, the east wind brought the locusts.**

The Lord brought an east wind: directional wind plays a prominent part in scriptural events. The east wind caused blight upon crops (Gen. 41:6), withered the gourd of Jonah (Jon. 4:8), and in general, typified the judgment of God (cf. Hos. 13:15; Ezek. 17:10; 19:12). Here, the east wind brings the devastation of the locust swarms.

¹⁴ And the locusts went up over all the land of Egypt, and rested in all the coasts of Egypt: very grievous *were they*; before them there were no such locusts as they, neither after them shall be such. ¹⁵ For they covered the face of the whole earth, so that the land was darkened; and they did eat every herb of the land, and all the fruit of the trees which the hail had left: and there remained not any green thing in the trees, or in the herbs of the field, through all the land of Egypt.

All the fruit of the tress which the hail had left: true to the counselor's fears, the locust swarm would decimate the remaining agricultural system of Egypt. The army of locusts had devoured every green leaf and every herb in the field.

¹⁶ Then Pharaoh called for Moses and Aaron in haste; and he said, I have sinned against the LORD your God, and against you. ¹⁷ Now therefore forgive, I pray thee, my sin only this once, and intreat the LORD your God, that he may take away from me this death only. ¹⁸ And he went out from Pharaoh, and intreated the LORD.

I have sinned: In language similar to Pharaoh's declaration of sin following the destruction by hail, Pharaoh now extends his admission of wrongdoing to Moses. The **haste** is meant to relay the possibility of some agriculture remaining, only if Israel's God were to call off the locusts.

Now therefore forgive, I pray thee, my sin only this once: this is a completely new development in the plague narrative. It is important to recognize that the usage of sin and forgiveness do not express a New Testament association nor a covenant-based idea of the terms. Rather, Pharaoh is acknowledging wrongdoing, both against Israel's God and against Moses and Aaron, whom he had, just prior, forcibly cast out from his presence.

[19] And the LORD turned a mighty strong west wind, which took away the locusts, and cast them into the Red sea; there remained not one locust in all the coasts of Egypt. [20] But the LORD hardened Pharaoh's heart, so that he would not let the children of Israel go.

The Lord turned a mighty strong west wind: reacting to the pleas of Pharaoh, God sends a רוּחַ־יָם (*rūa yām*) meaning, *a wind of the sea*, casting the locusts into the Red Sea.

[21] And the LORD said unto Moses, Stretch out thine hand toward heaven, that there may be darkness over the land of Egypt, even darkness *which* may be felt. [22] And Moses stretched forth his hand toward heaven; and there was a thick darkness in all the land of Egypt three days: [23] They saw not one another, neither rose any from his place for three days: but all the children of Israel had light in their dwellings.

Darkness over the land: the third plague of the third cycle, following the pattern of the previous plagues, comes without warning to Pharaoh as Moses stretched his rod toward the heavens and a thick darkness overwhelmed the land (cf. Ps. 105:28). It was a **darkness that could be felt**, literally a *darkness of groping* (cf. Deut. 28:29), that so overwhelmed the Egyptians that **they saw not one another, neither rose any from his place for three days**. The suddenness and degree of darkness served a great blow to their perceptions of the sun-god, Ra. In contrast to the prevailing darkness that overwhelmed the Egyptians, the Israelites had **light in their dwellings**. Israel, in contrast to the prevailing darkness of Egypt, is bathed in light; a land of light in a world of darkness (cf. Matt. 5:14). Though uncertain, another possible explanation is that, due to the absence or mention of Goshen, as compared to the implied light in their dwellings, the light was only available within the physical habitations of the Israelites.

²⁴ **And Pharaoh called unto Moses, and said, Go ye, serve the LORD; only let your flocks and your herds be stayed: let your little ones also go with you.** ²⁵ **And Moses said, Thou must give us also sacrifices and burnt offerings, that we may sacrifice unto the LORD our God.**

Only let your flocks and herds be stayed: the futility of Pharaoh's resistance comes down to yet another compromise, this time allowing for women and children to depart but for the livestock of the Israelites to remain. Moses' response reveals to Pharaoh that no compromise will be made, but instead, Moses parlayed that Pharaoh would give to them sheep and oxen of his own for sacrifices and burnt offerings.

²⁶ **Our cattle also shall go with us; there shall not an hoof be left behind; for thereof must we take to serve the LORD our God; and we know not with what we must serve the LORD, until we come thither.** ²⁷ **But the LORD hardened Pharaoh's heart, and he would not let them go.** ²⁸ **And Pharaoh said unto him, Get thee from me, take heed to thyself, see my face no more; for in *that* day thou seest my face thou shalt die.** ²⁹ **And Moses said, Thou hast spoken well, I will see thy face again no more.**

Not a hoof shall be left behind: using a hyperbolic expression, Moses reveals that nothing of theirs shall be left behind; not one animal should remain.

I will see thy face again no more: this statement of finality is tied directly to the introduction of the following first three verses of chapter eleven, picking the dialogue back up in 11:4. Moses is correct in saying **I will see thy face again no more**, since the message given to Pharaoh after the death of the firstborn was more than likely delivered by envoy rather than Pharaoh himself (cf. Ex. 12:31).

Notes

CHAPTER ELEVEN

¹ And the LORD said unto Moses, Yet will I bring one plague *more* upon Pharaoh, and upon Egypt; afterwards he will let you go hence: when he shall let *you* go, he shall surely thrust you out hence altogether. ² Speak now in the ears of the people, and let every man borrow of his neighbour, and every woman of her neighbour, jewels of silver, and jewels of gold. ³ And the LORD gave the people favour in the sight of the Egyptians. Moreover the man Moses *was* very great in the land of Egypt, in the sight of Pharaoh's servants, and in the sight of the people.

The first three verses of chapter eleven function much like a parenthetical, following the final verse of chapter ten, allowing the reader to come to speed with the plans that God has already presented to Moses. Moses' agreement that **I will see thy face no more** (10:29), is back-dropped against the knowledge that, with the fruition of the last and final plague, Pharaoh would cast them out **hence altogether** (lit. *completely*). The irony of Pharaoh's attempt at compromise (10:24) is that God had already given the Israelites **favor in the sight of the Egyptians** and plans were underway to prepare for the gathering of goods, gold, and jewelry for their journey.

⁴ And Moses said, Thus saith the LORD, About midnight will I go out into the midst of Egypt: ⁵ And all the firstborn in the land of Egypt shall die, from the firstborn of Pharaoh that sitteth upon his throne, even unto the firstborn of the maidservant that *is* behind the mill; and all the firstborn of beasts. ⁶ And there shall be a great cry throughout all the land of Egypt, such as there was none like it, nor shall be like it any more.

About midnight…all the firstborn in the land of Egypt shall die: This final blow, revealed at the start of the Divine campaign (cf. Ex. 4:23), would attack the firstborn children and livestock of Egypt, regardless of one's social class or standing.

⁷ But against any of the children of Israel shall not a dog move his tongue, against man or beast: that ye may know how that the LORD doth put a difference between the Egyptians and Israel.

But against any of the children of Israel shall not a dog move his tongue: serving as a proverbial statement, God expresses that Israel will remain unmolested and Egypt would not, in any way, voice any more protest. Egypt's snarl and bark would be reduced to the cries and whimpers of a broken and defeated nation.

⁸ And all these thy servants shall come down unto me, and bow down themselves unto me, saying, Get thee out, and all the people that follow thee: and after that I will go out. And he went out from Pharaoh in a great anger.

Get thee out, and all the people that follow thee: alluding to the mixed multitude that would accompany

Israel out of Egypt (cf. Ex. 12:38), Moses prophesied that Pharaoh's court would come begging for Israel's departure after the death of the firstborn children. The allusion to extraneous people **that follow thee** most likely refers to the mixed multitude that accompanied Israel out of Egypt (12:38).

And he went out: Delivering this final message, Moses turned away and departed in great anger, אף, (*ap*), an abstract word in Hebrew meaning nose, which captures a Hebrew expression conveying the physical qualities of heavy breathing and flared nostrils; a visible and severe anger.

⁹ And the LORD said unto Moses, Pharaoh shall not hearken unto you; that my wonders may be multiplied in the land of Egypt. ¹⁰ And Moses and Aaron did all these wonders before Pharaoh: and the LORD hardened Pharaoh's heart, so that he would not let the children of Israel go out of his land.

Notes

CHAPTER TWELVE

¹ And the LORD spake unto Moses and Aaron in the land of Egypt, saying, ² This month *shall be* unto you the beginning of months: it *shall be* the first month of the year to you.

Marking a new historical epoch for the nation of Israel, God begins by declaring that this **month** חֹדֶשׁ, (*hōdesh*), literally, *new moon*, **is for you the beginning of months**. The break from Egypt would be so complete as to give the Israelites a new calendrical pattern, marking a new beginning. Moving from the Egyptian pattern of reconciling time, the Israelites would base their calendar primarily upon a lunar cycle. The commencement of each month would be marked by the physical observation of a new moon. This first new moon, called the **beginning** (lit. *head or chief*) **of months**, would lay the foundation for future generations that all calendrical observation would first begin with the month of deliverance (Nisan). Also, from this calendrical system the Jewish feasts and festivals would be reckoned, though future generations would also observe a civic calendar that would place the first day of the seventh month (Tishrei) as the Jewish New Year.

³ **Speak ye unto all the congregation of Israel, saying, In the tenth** *day* **of this month they shall take to them every man a lamb, according to the house of** *their* **fathers, a lamb for an house:** ⁴ **And if the household be too little for the lamb, let him and his neighbour next unto his house take** *it* **according to the number of the souls; every man according to his eating shall make your count for the lamb.**

On the tenth day of this month: the tenth day would only be specific to this first Passover. Coincidentally, it would be 40 years later on the 10th day of Nisan that Joshua would bring the people into the Promised Land (Josh. 4:19).

If the household be too little for the lamb: the activity of the Passover was a community event where a collective responsibility was taken to ensure that each family partook in consuming the lamb. If a family were too small to consume a whole lamb they were to join with a family nearest to them, lest any of the sacrifice remain.

⁵ **Your lamb shall be without blemish, a male of the first year: ye shall take** *it* **out from the sheep, or from the goats:** ⁶ **And ye shall keep it up until the fourteenth day of the same month: and the whole assembly of the congregation of Israel shall kill it in the evening.** ⁷ **And they shall take of the blood, and strike** *it* **on the two side posts and on the upper door post of the houses, wherein they shall eat it.**

Take of the blood: according to **12:22**, it would fall upon the elder male of each home to take a bound bundle of hyssop, dipped in the blood that had gathered in the basin from the slain lamb, and **strike** it against the upper and two side-posts of homes' door. Opinions vary as to the blood being within or without the home, but most likely the blood was applied on the external visible to the impending death-angel. In many ways, similar to the later activities of the alter found in the Tabernacle, the Israelites were essentially turning their homes into altars, upon which the sacrifice was slain and the powerful blood of life was applied.

[8] And they shall eat the flesh in that night, roast with fire, and unleavened bread; *and* **with bitter** *herbs* **they shall eat it. [9] Eat not of it raw, nor sodden at all with water, but roast** *with* **fire; his head with his legs, and with the purtenance thereof. [10] And ye shall let nothing of it remain until the morning; and that which remaineth of it until the morning ye shall burn with fire.**

Eat the flesh in that night: Consumption of the sacrifice and the instructions for its preparation are signally unique in the fact that it had to be *roast with fire; his head with his legs, and with the purtenance* (lit. *inwards*) thereof. One was not to dress the lamb in a manner of selective choice, but rather, the lamb was to be consumed wholly, without break or division (12:46), and if any of it remained, **ye shall burn it with fire**. Foreshadowing's of this sacrificial feast, the lamb and the blood, can be found in the person and work of Jesus Christ (cf. Rev. 13:9; Jn. 1:29,36; 6:53).

[11] And thus shall ye eat it; *with* **your loins girded, your shoes on your feet, and your staff in your hand; and ye shall eat it in haste: it** *is* **the LORD'S passover.[12] For I will pass through the land of Egypt this night, and will smite all the firstborn in the land of Egypt, both man and**

88

beast; and against all the gods of Egypt I will execute judgment: I *am* the LORD.[13] And the blood shall be to you for a token upon the houses where ye *are*: and when I see the blood, I will pass over you, and the plague shall not be upon you to destroy *you*, when I smite the land of Egypt.

The blood shall be to you for a token: the blood of the lamb would serve as a **token** (lit. *sign*) to the Lord that substitution had been made for those within the home thus causing the death angel to pass over the house. In the past plagues, God had been the one to establish the redemptive severing or distinguishing between Israel and Egypt. However, with the impending death of the firstborn children, Israel was saddled with the responsibility to ensure the redemptive barrier be secured via their application of the blood of the lamb upon the lintels and posts of the door. While Israel had maintained a certain degree of immunity in many of the former plagues, no such luxury was permitted in this instance. Egyptian or Israelite, blood must be applied or judgment would not be passed over.

[14] And this day shall be unto you for a memorial; and ye shall keep it a feast to the LORD throughout your generations; ye shall keep it a feast by an ordinance for ever. [15] Seven days shall ye eat unleavened bread; even the first day ye shall put away leaven out of your houses: for whosoever eateth leavened bread from the first day until the seventh day, that soul shall be cut off from Israel. [16] And in the first day *there shall be* an holy convocation, and in the seventh day there shall be an holy convocation to you; no manner of work shall be done in them, save *that* which every man must eat, that only may be done of you. [17] And ye shall observe

the feast of unleavened bread; for in this selfsame day have I brought your armies out of the land of Egypt: therefore shall ye observe this day in your generations by an ordinance for ever. ¹⁸ In the first *month*, on the fourteenth day of the month at even, ye shall eat unleavened bread, until the one and twentieth day of the month at even. ¹⁹ Seven days shall there be no leaven found in your houses: for whosoever eateth that which is leavened, even that soul shall be cut off from the congregation of Israel, whether he be a stranger, or born in the land. ²⁰ Ye shall eat nothing leavened; in all your habitations shall ye eat unleavened bread.

Seven days shall ye eat unleavened bread: the instructions for future observations of the Passover, while reenacting several of the key elements of the first Passover, would not be limited to one day, but rather, initiate an entire week commonly known as the *Feast of Unleavened Bread*. It would be **between the evenings**, beginning on the 14th, that the lamb would be slain and prepared. Then, on the 15th, the Feast of Unleavened Bread would begin concurrent with the Passover meal. The 15th, the first day of the feast, was a **holy convocation** (a Sabbath) where work was not allowed, **except which every man must eat** (cf. Deut. 16:1-8).

²¹ Then Moses called for all the elders of Israel, and said unto them, Draw out and take you a lamb according to your families, and kill the passover. ²² And ye shall take a bunch of hyssop, and dip *it* in the blood that *is* in the bason, and strike the lintel and the two side posts with the blood that *is* in the bason; and none of you shall go out at the door of his house until the morning. ²³ For the LORD will pass through to smite the Egyptians; and

when he seeth the blood upon the lintel, and on the two side posts, the LORD will pass over the door, and will not suffer the destroyer to come in unto your houses to smite *you*. ²⁴ And ye shall observe this thing for an ordinance to thee and to thy sons for ever. ²⁵ And it shall come to pass, when ye be come to the land which the LORD will give you, according as he hath promised, that ye shall keep this service. ²⁶ And it shall come to pass, when your children shall say unto you, What mean ye by this service? ²⁷ That ye shall say, It is the sacrifice of the LORD'S passover, who passed over the houses of the children of Israel in Egypt, when he smote the Egyptians, and delivered our houses. And the people bowed the head and worshipped.

Then Moses called for all the elders: Conveying instructions to prepare for the coming destroyer that would visit Egypt, Moses does not inform the people of the future observations and ordinances God had given. Instead, focusing upon the hour of impending deliverance he relays to them the generational responsibility to always keep the Passover as a reminder of what God was going to do the coming evening. Recognizing that their liberation was so soon, the people respond with humility and worship.

²⁸ And the children of Israel went away, and did as the LORD had commanded Moses and Aaron, so did they. ²⁹ And it came to pass, that at midnight the LORD smote all the firstborn in the land of Egypt, from the firstborn of Pharaoh that sat on his throne unto the firstborn of the captive that *was* in the dungeon; and all the firstborn of cattle. ³⁰ And Pharaoh rose up in the night, he, and all his servants, and all the Egyptians; and there was a great cry in Egypt; for *there was* not a house where *there was*

not one dead. ³¹ **And he called for Moses and Aaron by night, and said, Rise up,** *and* **get you forth from among my people, both ye and the children of Israel; and go, serve the LORD, as ye have said.** ³² **Also take your flocks and your herds, as ye have said, and be gone; and bless me also.**

It came to pass at midnight: that is to say, between the 14th and 15th when the children of Israel had already prepared and were partaking of the Passover Feast, fully clothed and ready to depart in haste.

Bless me also: a unique and unexpected statement is uttered by Pharaoh in the request of **bless me also**. This brings to mind the act of blessing that had occurred between Jacob, the father of Joseph, and the then reigning Pharaoh (cf. Gen. 47:10). Now, just as then, the oppressive and formerly unrelenting Pharaoh seeks the blessing of Moses.

³³ **And the Egyptians were urgent upon the people, that they might send them out of the land in haste; for they said, We** *be* **all dead** *men*. ³⁴ **And the people took their dough before it was leavened, their kneadingtroughs being bound up in their clothes upon their shoulders.**

Took dough…before it was leavened: having only eaten unleavened bread the night before, the dough was placed in **kneadingtroughs**, vessels that were used to store dough that had been mixed with leaven. This dough, due to the haste of the Israelites, was yet to be mixed with yeast. The future observations of the Feast of Unleavened Bread would certainly summon to mind the haste that did not allow for the bread to rise.

³⁵ And the children of Israel did according to the word of Moses; and they borrowed of the Egyptians jewels of silver, and jewels of gold, and raiment: ³⁶ And the LORD gave the people favour in the sight of the Egyptians, so that they lent unto them *such things as they required*. And they spoiled the Egyptians. ³⁷ And the children of Israel journeyed from Rameses to Succoth, about six hundred thousand on foot *that were* men, beside children.

Children of Israel journeyed from Ramses to Succoth: the location of Succoth is undetermined, though the route of their journey to Sinai can be established. Succoth means *booths* or *tents* and could merely be the name the location received after their first encampment as a nation.

About 600,000, beside children: thirteen months later, the men twenty-years of age and above, able-bodied and fit for battle were numbered to be 603,550 (cf. Num. 1:45-46). 600,000 is also cited in Numbers 11:21 and another census, almost 40 years later revealed 601, 730 males twenty years and up (cf. Num. 26:51). These staggering statistics, even great if one includes the elderly, women, and children, lead many to believe that the congregation of Israel could have easily numbered upwards of 2 million, including the mixed multitude that accompanied them. This figure agrees with the fears of Pharaoh and the general observation that the Israelite people were more numerous than his own (cf. Ex. 1:9). Another possible interpretation involves the Hebrew word for thousand אֶלֶף (*'eleph*), which can also mean *company or unit*. This interpretation has been used to reconcile problems some have with so large a company as 2 million, thus bringing the number much lower.

³⁸ And a mixed multitude went up also with them; and flocks, and herds, *even* very much cattle. ³⁹ And they baked unleavened cakes of the dough which they brought forth out of Egypt, for it was not leavened; because they were thrust out of Egypt, and could not tarry, neither had they prepared for themselves any victual.

A mixed multitude went up also: scripture is silent regarding the identity of this multitude. One thing that stands out in the progression of the wandering narrative is that they were often the fountainhead of rebellious desire (cf. Num. 11:4).

⁴⁰ Now the sojourning of the children of Israel, who dwelt in Egypt, *was* four hundred and thirty years. ⁴¹ And it came to pass at the end of the four hundred and thirty years, even the selfsame day it came to pass, that all the hosts of the LORD went out from the land of Egypt. ⁴² It *is* a night to be much observed unto the LORD for bringing them out from the land of Egypt: this *is* that night of the LORD to be observed of all the children of Israel in their generations.

The sojourning of the children of Israel...was four hundred and thirty years: reiterated by the Apostle Paul in Galatians 3:17, the number 430 is likely a combination of the years of bondage (215) and the patriarchal years, beginning with Abraham's arrival into Canaan ending with Jacob's arrival into Egypt (215). According to Acts 7:6, a figure of 400 is given, most likely focusing on the four generations that would fulfill the iniquity of the Amorites (cf. Gen. 15:16).

⁴³ And the LORD said unto Moses and Aaron, This is the ordinance of the passover: There shall no stranger

eat thereof: ⁴⁴ But every man's servant that is bought for money, when thou hast circumcised him, then shall he eat thereof. ⁴⁵ A foreigner and an hired servant shall not eat thereof. ⁴⁶ In one house shall it be eaten; thou shalt not carry forth ought of the flesh abroad out of the house; neither shall ye break a bone thereof. ⁴⁷ All the congregation of Israel shall keep it. ⁴⁸ And when a stranger shall sojourn with thee, and will keep the passover to the LORD, let all his males be circumcised, and then let him come near and keep it; and he shall be as one that is born in the land: for no uncircumcised person shall eat thereof. ⁴⁹ One law shall be to him that is homeborn, and unto the stranger that sojourneth among you. ⁵⁰ Thus did all the children of Israel; as the LORD commanded Moses and Aaron, so did they. ⁵¹ And it came to pass the selfsame day, *that* the LORD did bring the children of Israel out of the land of Egypt by their armies.

No stranger shall eat thereof: the ordinances concerning participation in the Passover strictly forbid the foreigner and hired servants. The benchmark of participation for the home born servant and the sojourning stranger was circumcision. Scriptural evidence lends toward the failure to circumcise while in the wilderness (cf. Josh. 5:5) which opens up a unique perceptive on the observation of the Passover. It is evident from other scriptures that Passover observation was an issue (cf. Num. 9:10).

Notes

CHAPTER 13

¹ And the LORD spake unto Moses, saying, ² Sanctify unto me all the firstborn, whatsoever openeth the womb among the children of Israel, *both* of man and of beast: it *is* mine. ³ And Moses said unto the people, Remember this day, in which ye came out from Egypt, out of the house of bondage; for by strength of hand the LORD brought you out from this *place*: there shall no leavened bread be eaten. ⁴ This day came ye out in the month Abib. ⁵ And it shall be when the LORD shall bring thee into the land of the Canaanites, and the Hittites, and the Amorites, and the Hivites, and the Jebusites, which he sware unto thy fathers to give thee, a land flowing with milk and honey, that thou shalt keep this service in this month. ⁶ Seven days thou shalt eat unleavened bread, and in the seventh day *shall be* a feast to the LORD. ⁷ Unleavened bread shall be eaten seven days; and there shall no leavened bread be seen with thee, neither shall there be leaven seen with thee in all thy quarters. ⁸ And thou shalt shew thy son in that day, saying, *This is done* because of that *which* the LORD did unto me when I came forth out of Egypt.

No leavened bread be seen with thee: Here, Moses relays the instructions for the Feast of Unleavened

Bread that God had given prior (12:14-20). Moses further elaborates that, not only was leaven to be absent within the home, but also their quarters (lit. borders).

⁹ **And it shall be for a sign unto thee upon thine hand, and for a memorial between thine eyes, that the LORD'S law may be in thy mouth: for with a strong hand hath the LORD brought thee out of Egypt. ¹⁰ Thou shalt therefore keep this ordinance in his season from year to year.**

Upon thine hand, and for a memorial between thine eyes: the practice of wearing *tephillin*, also called phylacteries in the New Testament (cf. Mat. 23:5), is believed to have originated from this initial ordinance. Four specific portions of the Torah (Ex. 13:1-10; 11-16; Deut. 6:4-9; 11:13-21) were to be placed within two black boxes that were tied, one around the head with box centered on the forehead and the other wrapped around the arm seven times and centered upon the top of the hand.

¹¹ **And it shall be when the LORD shall bring thee into the land of the Canaanites, as he sware unto thee and to thy fathers, and shall give it thee, ¹² That thou shalt set apart unto the LORD all that openeth the matrix, and every firstling that cometh of a beast which thou hast; the males *shall be* the LORD'S. ¹³ And every firstling of an ass thou shalt redeem with a lamb; and if thou wilt not redeem it, then thou shalt break his neck: and all the firstborn of man among thy children shalt thou redeem.**

Every firstling of an ass thou shalt redeem with a lamb: the *laws of redemption* are expressed here in relation to the firstborn of man and animal. The price of redemption for the firstborn male children of Israel was set at five shekels (cf. Num. 18:16). Here, while other livestock could be redeemed by the shekel, the ass was to be redeemed by a lamb. If not, they were to break the neck of the ass. There is a unique parallel being drawn that is contrasting the events of Passover and the unclean ass. Just as Israel's firstborn had to be redeemed with a lamb on the Passover night to avoid being smitten, so did the ass have to be redeemed with a lamb, lest its neck be broken. As one progresses into the New Covenant through Jesus Christ, one recognizes redemption no longer through corruptible things, such as gold and silver, but through the blood of Jesus Christ, a lamb without blemish (cf. I Pet. 1:18).

14 And it shall be when thy son asketh thee in time to come, saying, What *is* this? that thou shalt say unto him, By strength of hand the LORD brought us out from Egypt, from the house of bondage: 15 And it came to pass, when Pharaoh would hardly let us go, that the LORD slew all the firstborn in the land of Egypt, both the firstborn of man, and the firstborn of beast: therefore I sacrifice to the LORD all that openeth the matrix, being males; but all the firstborn of my children I redeem. 16 And it shall be for a token upon thine hand, and for frontlets between thine eyes: for by strength of hand the LORD brought us forth out of Egypt. 17 And it came to pass, when Pharaoh had let the people go, that God led them not *through* the way of the land of the Philistines, although that *was* near; for God said, Lest peradventure the people repent when they see war, and they return to Egypt: 18 But God led the people about, *through* the way of the wilderness of the Red sea: and the children of Israel went up harnessed out of the land of Egypt.

God led them not through the way of the land of the Philistines: several routes would have proven more direct, the most feasible route the **way of the land of the Philistines**, nearest their encampment at Succoth, one that would have led them to the very heart of Canaan. Instead, **Peradventure the people repent when they see war**, God led them through the wilderness of the Red Sea. It should be noted that scripture doesn't emphasize an *engagement in war*, but rather, *when they see* (lit. *perceive*) *war*. God recognized that, not the battle itself, but even the mere perception of a possible battle would prove too daunting for this newly liberated people. Ironically, even after the many miracles and direct invention of God that accompanied the nation of Israel, they would still exemplify a desire to return to Egypt at the mere *perception* of future struggles and battles (cf. Num. 14:4).

They went up harnessed: that is to say, they went up in *orderly array*, organized with a military precision of rank. The emphasis here is to indicate that they did not leave in a jumbled, disorganized mass.

[19] **And Moses took the bones of Joseph with him: for he had straitly sworn the children of Israel, saying, God will surely visit you; and ye shall carry up my bones away hence with you.**

Moses took the bones of Joseph: fulfilling the request of Joseph (Gen. 50:25), Moses takes the bones of Joseph and, possibly the remains of Jacob's other sons (Acts 7:15-16), and secures their safe departure from Egypt. It wouldn't be until the subsequent generation, and the forty years of wilderness wandering, that the bones of Joseph would be laid to rest in Shechem (Josh. 24:32).

[20] And they took their journey from Succoth, and encamped in Etham, in the edge of the wilderness. 21 And the LORD went before them by day in a pillar of a cloud, to lead them the way; and by night in a pillar of fire, to give them light; to go by day and night: 22 He took not away the pillar of the cloud by day, nor the pillar of fire by night, *from* before the people.

The Lord went before them: utilizing the pillar of cloud and fire, God acted as shepherd and guide to the congregation of Israel, enabling them to travel by day and night.

Notes

CHAPTER 14

¹ And the LORD spake unto Moses, saying, ² Speak unto the children of Israel, that they turn and encamp before Pihahiroth, between Migdol and the sea, over against Baalzephon: before it shall ye encamp by the sea. ³ For Pharaoh will say of the children of Israel, They *are* entangled in the land, the wilderness hath shut them in. ⁴ And I will harden Pharaoh's heart, that he shall follow after them; and I will be honoured upon Pharaoh, and upon all his host; that the Egyptians may know that I *am* the LORD. And they did so. ⁵ And it was told the king of Egypt that the people fled: and the heart of Pharaoh and of his servants was turned against the people, and they said, Why have we done this, that we have let Israel go from serving us? ⁶ And he made ready his chariot, and took his people with him:

Turn and encamp…ye shall encamp by the sea: the command to turn from their southeastern journey to encamp by the Sea set into motion a divine plan that would cause Pharaoh to think **they are entangled** (lit. *perplexed*) **in the land**. This ploy, with Israel as the bait, would draw Pharaoh and his armies out of Egypt so that God could execute a final act of judgment, and establish His identity in Egypt (vs. 17-18). God would be **honoured upon** (lit. *receive glory over*) Pharaoh and the armies of Egypt.

⁷ **And he took six hundred chosen chariots, and all the chariots of Egypt, and captains over every one of them.** ⁸ **And the LORD hardened the heart of Pharaoh king of Egypt, and he pursued after the children of Israel: and the children of Israel went out with an high hand.**

He took six hundred chosen chariots, and all the chariots of Egypt, and captains over every one of them: it should be noted that both the choice chariots and all the chariots of Egypt were employed. Each chariot would have been manned by a minimum of two men, harnessed to no less than two horses, and would have accompanied a large contingency of cavalry and infantry (vs. 9, 17). While this number seems slight in contrast to the numbers of Israel, the overwhelming offensive might of Egypt would have easily turned the battle into their favour and decimated Israel.

9 But the Egyptians pursued after them, all the horses *and* chariots of Pharaoh, and his horsemen, and his army, and overtook them encamping by the sea, beside Pihahiroth, before Baalzephon. 10 And when Pharaoh drew nigh, the children of Israel lifted up their eyes, and, behold, the Egyptians marched after them; and they were sore afraid: and the children of Israel cried out unto the LORD. 11 And they said unto Moses, Because *there were* no graves in Egypt, hast thou taken us away to die in the wilderness? wherefore hast thou dealt thus with us, to carry us forth out of Egypt? 12 Is not this the word that we did tell thee in Egypt, saying, Let us alone, that we may serve the Egyptians? For *it had been* better for us to serve the Egyptians, than that we should die in the wilderness.

Is not this the word that we did tell thee in Egypt: an insight as to the original opposition toward Moses and Aaron is revealed in that they, at some point, had merely wished to be let alone that they may **serve the Egyptians**. Now, the fear of dying overwhelmed their memory of harsh labor.

[13] And Moses said unto the people, Fear ye not, stand still, and see the salvation of the LORD, which he will shew to you to day: for the Egyptians whom ye have seen to day, ye shall see them again no more for ever. [14] The LORD shall fight for you, and ye shall hold your peace. [15] And the LORD said unto Moses, Wherefore criest thou unto me? speak unto the children of Israel, that they go forward: [16] But lift thou up thy rod, and stretch out thine hand over the sea, and divide it: and the children of Israel shall go on dry *ground* through the midst of the sea. [17] And I, behold, I will harden the hearts of the Egyptians, and they shall follow them: and I will get me honour upon Pharaoh, and upon all his host, upon his chariots, and upon his horsemen. [18] And the Egyptians shall know that I *am* the LORD, when I have gotten me honour upon Pharaoh, upon his chariots, and upon his horsemen.

I will harden the hearts of the Egyptians: here the acting of hardening is חָזַק (*hāzaq*) meaning *strengthened*, which implies God would bolster the courage of the Egyptians to overlook the awesome sight of the divided waters and give pursuit with the design of swallowing them up.

[19] And the angel of God, which went before the camp of Israel, removed and went behind them; and the pillar of the cloud went from before their face, and stood behind them:

And the angel of God…removed and went behind them: the agency of God's manifestation in the form of a pillar of cloud moved from the frontal position, where it acted as the guiding shepherd to the rear position, where it would act as a following rear guard (cf. Isa 63:11-13). Though later scripture would seem to imply that the pillar of fire was replaced by the pillar of cloud during specific times, both seem to be in operation at this given moment since darkness was behind and light was ahead.

[20] And it came between the camp of the Egyptians and the camp of Israel; and it was a cloud and darkness to them, but it gave light by night *to these*: so that the one came not near the other all the night.

It was a cloud and darkness to them, but it gave light by night to these: with an event of darkness that is similar to the events of the 9th plague, the Israelites are provided light while the Egyptians are completely halted by a total obscurity that disabled them from mounting any form of militant pursuit. This incident, as well the 9th plague, summon to mind the common motif throughout scriptures where God's children are associated with light and His enemies are associated with darkness (cf. Eph. 5:8; 1 Thess. 5:5).

[21] And Moses stretched out his hand over the sea; and the LORD caused the sea to go *back* by a strong east wind all that night, and made the sea dry *land*, and the waters were divided. [22] And the children of Israel went into the midst of the sea upon the dry *ground*: and the waters *were* a wall unto them on their right hand, and on their left.

A strong east wind that brought the locusts would now

blow all through the night. The correlation between the blowing wind, the dry sea bed, and the divided waters cannot be overlooked. In other words, it was a commissioned wind that opened an impossible path that allowed for the miraculous progress of the nation of Israel.

23 And the Egyptians pursued, and went in after them to the midst of the sea, *even* all Pharaoh's horses, his chariots, and his horsemen. 24 And it came to pass, that in the morning watch the LORD looked unto the host of the Egyptians through the pillar of fire and of the cloud, and troubled the host of the Egyptians, 25 And took off their chariot wheels, that they drave them heavily: so that the Egyptians said, Let us flee from the face of Israel; for the LORD fighteth for them against the Egyptians.

The Egyptians pursued: it would seem, after Israel had made it to the other side, that the cloud was lifted and the Egyptians, thinking the path to remain, pursued. However, **in the morning watch the Lord looked unto the host of the Egyptians through the pillar of fire and of the cloud:** that is to say, God discomfited them with a mighty, celestial storm that involved tremendous rain, wind, and lightening (cf. Ps. 18:14-15; II Sam 22:15). The pounding, hurricane strength storm caused the wheels of the chariots to get stuck in the mud and, with the panic of Egyptians and horses, were ripped off in their effort to flee. Abandoning their now useless chariots, the Egyptians thought to flee through the muck and mire on foot, recognizing the storm to be supernatural. Indeed, God was receiving glory over them.

26 And the LORD said unto Moses, Stretch out thine hand over the sea, that the waters may come again

upon the Egyptians, upon their chariots, and upon their horsemen. ²⁷ And Moses stretched forth his hand over the sea, and the sea returned to his strength when the morning appeared; and the Egyptians fled against it; and the LORD overthrew the Egyptians in the midst of the sea. ²⁸ And the waters returned, and covered the chariots, and the horsemen, *and* all the host of Pharaoh that came into the sea after them; there remained not so much as one of them.

The waters may come again: The irony of this scenario calls to mind the casting of the Hebrew male infants into the Nile River (1:22). Now, battling to escape the mud that impeded their escape, the horses and armies of Egypt watched in terror as the waters begin to rise and the river, having stood as walls on either side, **returned to his strength** (lit. *turn again to flow*) and the Lord **overthrew**, נִעֵר (*na'ar*), meaning to shake off (cf. Job. 39:13), the Egyptians into the deeper part of the sea completely obliterating their entire host.

²⁹ But the children of Israel walked upon dry land in the midst of the sea; and the waters *were* a wall unto them on their right hand, and on their left. ³⁰ Thus the LORD saved Israel that day out of the hand of the Egyptians; and Israel saw the Egyptians dead upon the sea shore. ³¹ And Israel saw that great work which the LORD did upon the Egyptians: and the people feared the LORD, and believed the LORD, and his servant Moses.

Notes

CHAPTER 15

¹ **Then sang Moses and the children of Israel this song unto the LORD, and spake, saying, I will sing unto the LORD, for he hath triumphed gloriously: the horse and his rider hath he thrown into the sea.**

Then sang Moses...this song: This is one of three compositions by Moses (cf. Deut. 31:22; Ps. 90). Commonly referred to as the Song of the Sea, it should not be confused with the Song of Moses (Deut. 31:22), that is also sung in the Apocalyptic vision of John (Rev. 15:3). The overall theme of the Song of the Sea is one of triumph, both present and of things future. Ten times YHWH is mentioned, emphasizing His power of redemption and deliverance. The composition and orchestration of songs would become a common response throughout scripture following moments of victory, deliverance, or divine intervention (cf. Judges 5; 1 Sam. 2; 2 Sam 22).

² **The LORD *is* my strength and song, and he is become my salvation: he *is* my God, and I will prepare him an habitation; my father's God, and I will exalt him. ³ The LORD *is* a man of war: the LORD *is* his name. ⁴ Pharaoh's chariots and his host hath he cast into the sea: his chosen**

captains also are drowned in the Red sea. ⁵ The depths have covered them: they sank into the bottom as a stone. ⁶ Thy right hand, O LORD, is become glorious in power: thy right hand, O LORD, hath dashed in pieces the enemy. ⁷ And in the greatness of thine excellency thou hast overthrown them that rose up against thee: thou sentest forth thy wrath, *which* consumed them as stubble. ⁸ And with the blast of thy nostrils the waters were gathered together, the floods stood upright as an heap, *and* the depths were congealed in the heart of the sea. ⁹ The enemy said, I will pursue, I will overtake, I will divide the spoil; my lust shall be satisfied upon them; I will draw my sword, my hand shall destroy them. ¹⁰ Thou didst blow with thy wind, the sea covered them: they sank as lead in the mighty waters.

Similar Psalms express this event in the form of hymn (cf. Psa. 66:5-6; 77:15-21). These Psalms, while not expressing the drowning of the Egyptians, focus more upon God's triumph over nature (the sea drying up). Other instances in scripture, echoing the same theme of the Song of the Sea, focus on the historical act of what God had done from the viewpoint of saving the people of Israel via the waters God triumphed over (cf. Josh 4:22-28). In Isaiah, the account at the Red Sea is expressed in ancient mythological language where God deals with a revolting sea, a mythological sea monster called Rahab, and a dragon. God triumphs over all three, cutting Rahab into pieces while piercing the heart of the dragon (lit. crocodile) so that the ransomed could pass over (Isa. 51:9-10).

¹¹ Who *is* like unto thee, O LORD, among the gods? who *is* like thee, glorious in holiness, fearful *in* praises, doing wonders? ¹² Thou stretchedst out thy right hand,

the earth swallowed them. ⁱ³ Thou in thy mercy hast led forth the people *which* thou hast redeemed: thou hast guided *them* in thy strength unto thy holy habitation. ¹⁴ The people shall hear, *and* be afraid: sorrow shall take hold on the inhabitants of Palestina. ¹⁵ Then the dukes of Edom shall be amazed; the mighty men of Moab, trembling shall take hold upon them; all the inhabitants of Canaan shall melt away. ¹⁶ Fear and dread shall fall upon them; by the greatness of thine arm they shall be *as* still as a stone; till thy people pass over, O LORD, till the people pass over, *which* thou hast purchased. ¹⁷ Thou shalt bring them in, and plant them in the mountain of thine inheritance, in the place, O LORD, *which* thou hast made for thee to dwell in, *in* the Sanctuary, O Lord, *which* thy hands have established. ¹⁸ The LORD shall reign for ever and ever. ¹⁹ For the horse of Pharaoh went in with his chariots and with his horsemen into the sea, and the LORD brought again the waters of the sea upon them; but the children of Israel went on dry *land* in the midst of the sea.

²⁰ And Miriam the prophetess, the sister of Aaron, took a timbrel in her hand; and all the women went out after her with timbrels and with dances. ²¹ And Miriam answered them, Sing ye to the LORD, for he hath triumphed gloriously; the horse and his rider hath he thrown into the sea.

Miriam answered them: repeating the first strophe of the song, Miriam and the women replied **with timbrels** (tambourines) **and with dances**, a practice not isolated to this incident alone (cf. Judg. 11:34; I Sam. 18:6). Later prophetic literature would cast a picture similar to these events, though speaking of a future return of the redeemed of the Lord to Zion (cf. Isa. 51:9-11).

²² **So Moses brought Israel from the Red sea, and they went out into the wilderness of Shur; and they went three days in the wilderness, and found no water.** ²³ **And when they came to Marah, they could not drink of the waters of Marah, for they were bitter: therefore the name of it was called Marah.**

They went three days...and found no water: the absence of water following a journey covering approximately 30-45 miles would have greatly taxed the resources of so large a group, including the livestock that accompanied them. The namesake of the location, **Marah**, reflected the conditions of the water, **for they were bitter**, perhaps due to large quantities of salt that would have rendered the water undrinkable.

²⁴ **And the people murmured against Moses, saying, What shall we drink?** ²⁵ **And he cried unto the LORD; and the LORD shewed him a tree, *which* when he had cast into the waters, the waters were made sweet: there he made for them a statute and an ordinance, and there he proved them,** ²⁶ **And said, If thou wilt diligently hearken to the voice of the LORD thy God, and wilt do that which is right in his sight, and wilt give ear to his commandments, and keep all his statutes, I will put none of these diseases upon thee, which I have brought upon the Egyptians: for I *am* the LORD that healeth thee.** ²⁷ **And they came to Elim, where *were* twelve wells of water, and threescore and ten palm trees: and they encamped there by the waters.**

The Lord shewed him a tree: some discussion has attempted to identify the tree as a mangrove, due to its known qualities that lend toward desalination. However, in light of God's known actions of taking natural resources and changing their properties (cf. Jn. 2:9; II Kings 2:19-22), a natural explanation may not be necessary.

There he proved them: God's act of proving, הָסָנ (*nāsâ*), a word that signifies *putting to the test*, is something that would not be relegated to this instance alone. Setting forth a statute and ordinance the conditional promise of God (*protecting them from the diseases placed upon Egypt*) could only be secured by the people *if* they would **diligently hearken to His voice, do what is right in His sight, give hear to His commandments, and keep all His statues**. The turning of bitter waters sweet served as a direct example of **the Lord that healeth thee**; a real-world illustration of God's sheltering power to those that would adhere to His word.

Notes

CHAPTER 16

¹ And they took their journey from Elim, and all the congregation of the children of Israel came unto the wilderness of Sin, which *is* between Elim and Sinai, on the fifteenth day of the second month after their departing out of the land of Egypt. ² And the whole congregation of the children of Israel murmured against Moses and Aaron in the wilderness: ³ And the children of Israel said unto them, Would to God we had died by the hand of the LORD in the land of Egypt, when we sat by the flesh pots, *and* when we did eat bread to the full; for ye have brought us forth into this wilderness, to kill this whole assembly with hunger.

When we sat by the flesh pots: The idea of **eating bread to the full** may have existed under the regime of the Pharaoh that knew Joseph, but not the one that followed. Exaggeration is expressed by the murmuring people, going as far as to accuse Moses and Aaron of bringing them out of Egypt **to kill** the **whole assembly with hunger**. Considering the presence of a large company of livestock (cf. 12:38; 18:3) one should wonder why such a grievance is raised. One possible solution for this would be that the livestock, such as the gold, silver, and jewels, were taken possession of by individuals and not a shared property. This would result in many of the camp not having livestock or ample food stores to fall back on, especially since the unleavened dough they had departed Egypt with (see 12:34) would have been consumed by this time.

⁴ Then said the LORD unto Moses, Behold, I will rain bread from heaven for you; and the people shall go out and gather a certain rate every day, that I may prove them, whether they will walk in my law, or no. ⁵ And it shall come to pass, that on the sixth day they shall prepare *that* which they bring in; and it shall be twice as much as they gather daily.

Just as the bitter waters served to test the obedience of the congregation, the same would apply here. In this instance, after the miraculous bread fell from heaven, God would test them to see **whether they will walk in my law, or no**. God's provision came with the condition (*testing*) that every morning they were to gather **bread to the full** (lit. *bread to satiate*). Understanding the propensity for man to reach beyond what God designed for the day (cf. Matt. 6:11), the manna served a true test of their reliance and trust in God. Their visible trust in God would be revealed by their strict gathering for the day alone, believing God to provide for their tomorrow (cf. Matt. 6:25-26). Only on the Sabbath, whose details had yet to be given to them, were the people to gather an extra day's measure.

⁶ And Moses and Aaron said unto all the children of Israel, At even, then ye shall know that the LORD hath brought you out from the land of Egypt: ⁷ And in the morning, then ye shall see the glory of the LORD; for that he heareth your murmurings against the LORD: and

what *are* we, that ye murmur against us? ⁸ And Moses said, *This shall be*, when the LORD shall give you in the evening flesh to eat, and in the morning bread to the full; for that the LORD heareth your murmurings which ye murmur against him: and what are we? your murmurings *are* not against us, but against the LORD.

At even...ye shall know...and in the morning: Before the day would end the congregation of Israel would know that it was the Lord, not Moses and Aaron (v. 3), that had brought them out of Egypt to face the conditions they were in. By morning, they would also see with their own eyes the glory of the Lord and know that God had heard their murmuring thus realizing it wasn't Aaron and Moses with whom they murmured against. The true nature of their provocations with God are vividly captured by the Psalmist, revealing the stubborn and hardheaded nature of the children of Israel (Ps. 78:17-25). Yet, despite their contentious provocations God would still provide them with provision.

9 And Moses spake unto Aaron, Say unto all the congregation of the children of Israel, Come near before the LORD: for he hath heard your murmurings. 10 And it came to pass, as Aaron spake unto the whole congregation of the children of Israel, that they looked toward the wilderness, and, behold, the glory of the LORD appeared in the cloud. 11 And the LORD spake unto Moses, saying, 12 I have heard the murmurings of the children of Israel: speak unto them, saying, At even ye shall eat flesh, and in the morning ye shall be filled with bread; and ye shall know that I *am* the LORD your God. 13 And it came to pass, that at even the quails came up, and covered the camp: and in the morning the dew lay round about the host. 14 And when the dew that lay

was gone up, behold, upon the face of the wilderness *there lay* a small round thing, *as* small as the hoar frost on the ground. 15 And when the children of Israel saw *it*, they said one to another, It is manna: for they wist not what it *was*. And Moses said unto them, This *is* the bread which the LORD hath given you to eat. 16 This *is* the thing which the LORD hath commanded, Gather of it every man *according to* his eating, an omer for every man, according to the number of your persons; take ye every man for *them* which *are* in his tents.

It came to pass: true to God's word quail fell to the ground in the evening and in the morning and, after the dew had dissipated, there lay a **small round thing**: the meaning of *round thing*, מְחֻסְפָּס (*haspas*), is uncertain, though the Septuagint renders it as a *flake-like thing*. Expositors are not the only ones who remain uncertain as to the specific nature of the fine, flake-like substance for, when the Israelites saw it, they said one to another: **manna** (lit. *what* מָן (*mān*) *is it!*).

Gather…every man according to his eating: mirroring the verbiage of the Passover Lamb and the allotment for every family (Ex. 12:4-5), everyone man was to gather (by the omer) enough for those who dwelled within their tents. An **omer** was a dry-measure, *one-tenth of an ephah* (v. 36), estimated to be the equivalent of 5- 7 pints. English versions also translate **omer** עֹמֶר (*o'-mer*) in several scriptures as the sheaf (cf. Lev. 23:10,11,12,15; 24:19; Rut. 2:7), a unique connection when considering that when the manna ceased after moving in Canaan the children of Isreal were required to bring an omer (sheaf) of the firstfruits to be waved by the priesthood before the Lord (cf. Lev. 23:10).

[17] And the children of Israel did so, and gathered, some more, some less. [18] And when they did mete *it* with an omer, he that gathered much had nothing over, and he that gathered little had no lack; they gathered every man according to his eating. [19] And Moses said, Let no man leave of it till the morning. [20] Notwithstanding they hearkened not unto Moses; but some of them left of it until the morning, and it bred worms, and stank: and Moses was wroth with them.

Some of them left of it until the morning: the putrid remains of manna crawling with worms (lit. *maggots*) filled the tents of those who had failed to pass the testing of God (v. 4). Clearly, the stench within was enough to draw attention to those who had broken the commandment of God, a unique design by God to flush out the oath breakers. No one would enjoy the spoils of disobedience.

[21] And they gathered it every morning, every man according to his eating: and when the sun waxed hot, it melted. [22] And it came to pass, *that* on the sixth day they gathered twice as much bread, two omers for one *man*: and all the rulers of the congregation came and told Moses. [23] And he said unto them, This *is that* which the LORD hath said, To morrow is the rest of the holy sabbath unto the LORD: bake *that* which ye will bake *to day*, and seethe that ye will seethe; and that which remaineth over lay up for you to be kept until the morning. [24] And they laid it up till the morning, as Moses bade: and it did not stink, neither was there any worm therein. [25] And Moses said, Eat that to day; for to day *is* a sabbath unto the LORD: to day ye shall not find it in the field.

Today is a Sabbath unto the Lord: here, Israel's first

Sabbath observation following their departure from Egypt is associated with their gathering of manna and God's explicit restrictions on gathering the manna on the Sabbath day. Instead, a double-portion was to be gathered on the sixth day and they were to **bake** or **seeth** (lit. *boil*) what they needed for that specific day and store the rest for the Sabbath day following. This extra gathering, as it relates to the Sabbath, is remarkable when contrasted with those who gathered extra on days they were to only gather enough for the specific day at hand. Clearly, obedience, not the quantity of the manna, was the fundamental stipulation for God's preservation of the blessing.

[26] **Six days ye shall gather it; but on the seventh day,** *which is* **the sabbath, in it there shall be none.** [27] **And it came to pass,** *that* **there went out** *some* **of the people on the seventh day for to gather, and they found none.** [28] **And the LORD said unto Moses, How long refuse ye to keep my commandments and my laws?** [29] **See, for that the LORD hath given you the sabbath, therefore he giveth you on the sixth day the bread of two days; abide ye every man in his place, let no man go out of his place on the seventh day.** [30] **So the people rested on the seventh day.**

There went out some of the people on the seventh day: in contrast to the anger and rebuke of Moses at those who horded manna for the morrow (v. 20), it is God who expresses rebuke and anger at the disobedience of those who adhered not to the strict requirements of the sixth and seventh days as it related to the gathering of manna. Since the law had yet to be delivered, God is lenient toward those who would break this initial Sabbath. However, God would use the life sustaining substance of food to begin to habituate the children of Israel to the Sabbath of Rest.

[31] And the house of Israel called the name thereof Manna: and it *was* like coriander seed, white; and the taste of it *was* like wafers *made* with honey. [32] And Moses said, This is the thing which the LORD commandeth, Fill an omer of it to be kept for your generations; that they may see the bread wherewith I have fed you in the wilderness, when I brought you forth from the land of Egypt. [33] And Moses said unto Aaron, Take a pot, and put an omer full of manna therein, and lay it up before the LORD, to be kept for your generations. [34] As the LORD commanded Moses, so Aaron laid it up before the Testimony, to be kept.

Fill an omer...to be kept for your generation: until a later date, after the erection of the Tabernacle and the completion of the Ark of the Covenant, an omer of daily manna was gathered and stored in a pot overlaid with gold (Heb. 9:4). The power of God's preservation (over 40 years the manna remained in the pot, perhaps even until the building of Solomon's Temple) is contrasted with the futile attempts of the disobedient who had attempted to store up extra manna, only to find it full of maggots and stinking the following day. Interestingly, the concept of hidden manna is found in the book of Revelation and promised to be given to the overcomers of Pergamum (Rev. 2:17).

[35] And the children of Israel did eat manna forty years, until they came to a land inhabited; they did eat manna, until they came unto the borders of the land of Canaan. [36] Now an omer *is* the tenth *part* of an ephah.

Notes

CHAPTER 17

¹ And all the congregation of the children of Israel journeyed from the wilderness of Sin, after their journeys, according to the commandment of the LORD, and pitched in Rephidim: and *there was* no water for the people to drink. ² Wherefore the people did chide with Moses, and said, Give us water that we may drink. And Moses said unto them, Why chide ye with me? wherefore do ye tempt the LORD? ³ And the people thirsted there for water; and the people murmured against Moses, and said, Wherefore *is* this *that* thou hast brought us up out of Egypt, to kill us and our children and our cattle with thirst? ⁴ And Moses cried unto the LORD, saying, What shall I do unto this people? they be almost ready to stone me.

Pitched in Rephidim: moving from the wilderness of Sin, the congregation journeyed further toward Sinai and, **after their journeys** (lit. *stages or stations*), they pitched in **Rephidim**. Numbers 33:12-14 reveals two of the stages prior to Rephidim as Dophkah and Alush. It is supposed that Rephidim, whose location is uncertain, is thought to have been a valley that known to have waters during the rainy season. However, upon arriving, **there was no water for the people to drink**. The gravity of this moment grossly outweighed the previous instance of finding bitter waters for, in this case, there was a total lack of water.

The people did chide with Moses: not only did they murmur against Moses, they did **chide** (*strive*) with him. The severity of their angst against Moses was revealed in Moses' cry to God when he declared, **they be almost ready to stone me.**

⁵ **And the LORD said unto Moses, Go on before the people, and take with thee of the elders of Israel; and thy rod, wherewith thou smotest the river, take in thine hand, and go.**

Take... thy rod wherewith thou smotest the river: this event gives great clarity to a similar event recorded toward the end of Israel's journey (Num. 20:1-11). In this account, God specifies the rod that would accomplish the demand for water; **the rod wherewith thou smotest the river**. It was Moses' rod, not Aarons, which struck the river. A second instance involving the rock and the rod is found toward the end of their wilderness wandering. However, in the second instance found in Numbers, Moses is told to take the rod from before the Lord (Num. 20:9), clearly indicating Aaron's rod that had budded, which was to serve as a *token to the rebels* (cf. Num. 17:10).

⁶ **Behold, I will stand before thee there upon the rock in Horeb; and thou shalt smite the rock, and there shall come water out of it, that the people may drink. And Moses did so in the sight of the elders of Israel.**

I will stand before thee there upon the rock in Horeb: in the eyes of the elders (unlike the incident in Numbers

20 that was before all the people), Moses would strike the rock. This action would produce a miraculous flow of water out of the rock that, in turn, would fill the dry pathways in the valley of Rephidim, allowing for the people and livestock to drink. The typological connection between Jesus Christ and the rock in the wilderness (I Cor. 10:4) is a reminder that nothing that occurred during these events was not without a deep significance, both in the present and in the future.

[7] **And he called the name of the place Massah, and Meribah, because of the chiding of the children of Israel, and because they tempted the LORD, saying, Is the LORD among us, or not?**

He called the name of the place Massah and Meribah: here, the children of Israel had contended with God's man over water and put God to the test by declaring, is the Lord among us, or not. Because of this, the namesake of the location would reflect the twofold transgression of the people; **Massah**, meaning *temptation*, and **Meribah**, meaning *contention*. Another event, similar to this incident, is recorded at the end of their wilderness journey (Num. 20:1-11).

[8] **Then came Amalek, and fought with Israel in Rephidim.** [9] **And Moses said unto Joshua, Choose us out men, and go out, fight with Amalek: to morrow I will stand on the top of the hill with the rod of God in mine hand.** [10] **So Joshua did as Moses had said to him, and fought with Amalek: and Moses, Aaron, and Hur went up to the top of the hill.** [11] **And it came to pass, when Moses held up his hand, that Israel prevailed: and when he let down his hand, Amalek prevailed.** [12] **But Moses' hands** *were* **heavy; and they took a stone, and put** *it* **under him, and**

he sat thereon; and Aaron and Hur stayed up his hands, the one on the one side, and the other on the other side; and his hands were steady until the going down of the sun. [13] And Joshua discomfited Amalek and his people with the edge of the sword.

Then came Amalek: the Amalekites were a Bedouin tribe descended from Esau (Gen. 36:16). Per later scripture, Amalek, like a predator animal, had attacked the feeble at the rear of the congregation when Israel was the weariest (Deut. 25:17-19). This event would mark the first attack of the heathen world beyond Egypt against the called out, separated people of God.

Joshua, choose us out men: here, Joshua is mentioned for the first time in scripture, later identified as Moses' servant (Ex. 33:11). Joshua would later become the succeeding leader of the nation of Israel after the death of Moses.

When Moses held up his hand...Israel prevailed: the tide of the battle depended upon the rod remaining outstretched. The parallel between the condition of the battle and the outstretched rod is unique and possibly designed by God to demonstrate Israel's total dependence upon Him. Truly, life and death was in the mighty, outstretched hand of God (cf. Ex. 32:11; Deut. 4:34). With the help of Aaron and Hur, Moses was able to keep the rod extended in the air until the going down of the sun, at which point, Joshua **discomfited** (lit. *to cause one to lie prostrate*) the Amalekites.

[14] **And the LORD said unto Moses, Write this** *for* **a memorial in a book, and rehearse** *it* **in the ears of Joshua: for I will utterly put out the remembrance of**

Amalek from under heaven. ¹⁵ And Moses built an altar, and called the name of it Jehovahnissi: 16 For he said, Because the LORD hath sworn *that* the LORD *will have war with Amalek from generation to generation.*

Write this for a memorial in a book and rehearse it in the ears of Joshua: recorded in Deut. 25:17-19, the events of Amalek's attack were to serve as a memorial to future generations that would remind them of the declaration of God to **utterly put out the remembrance of Amalek**. The prophet Balaam, while posing a parable in regards to Amalek, would call them the *first of the nations* but declare that their latter end would be destruction forever (Num. 24:20). This memorialized promise would become the downfall of the future king of Saul when the commandment to *utterly destroy* Amalek was not met with obedience (I Sam. 15:3-18).

Moses built an altar: to memorialize the recent battle and the future war between God and Amalek, Moses built an altar and called over the altar the name of **Jehovahnissi** יְהֹוָה נִסִּי (*yehōwāh nissiy*), meaning ***the Lord is my Banner*** (cf. Ps. 60:4). Though English translations interpret Moses to name the altar, the declaration of the Lord is my Banner comes as a revelatory worship, calling out the name over the altar, based upon the events at Rephidim (cf. Gen. 28:18-19).

Notes

CHAPTER 18

¹ When Jethro, the priest of Midian, Moses' father in law, heard of all that God had done for Moses, and for Israel his people, *and* that the LORD had brought Israel out of Egypt; ² Then Jethro, Moses' father in law, took Zipporah, Moses' wife, after he had sent her back, ³ And her two sons; of which the name of the one *was* Gershom; for he said, I have been an alien in a strange land: ⁴ And the name of the other was Eliezer; for the God of my father, *said he, was* mine help, and delivered me from the sword of Pharaoh: ⁵ And Jethro, Moses' father in law, came with his sons and his wife unto Moses into the wilderness, where he encamped at the mount of God: ⁶ And he said unto Moses, I thy father in law Jethro am come unto thee, and thy wife, and her two sons with her. ⁷ And Moses went out to meet his father in law, and did obeisance, and kissed him; and they asked each other of *their* welfare; and they came into the tent.

Took Zipporah, Moses' wife...and her two sons: scripture heretofore had not mentioned the placement or instructions revolving around Moses' family after the incident of Zipporah's hasty circumcision of their son. Clearly, desiring to focus on the task of confronting Pharaoh, Moses had sent his wife and children back to Jethro until such a time allowed for them to return.

There is evidence to indicate that the arrival of Jethro and Moses' family are not recorded within the chronological structure of Exodus. It is more than likely that the events described here took place as the people were about to depart from Sinai (cf. Num. 11:14-17; Deut. 1:7-14). A couple other reasons for this are as follows:

1. Here (vs 5) is reveals that Jethro arrives when they were **encamped at the mount of God**. However, based on Exodus 19:1-2, they were yet to arrive and encamp at the mount of God.
2. The contention that arose in regards to Zipporah by Miriam and Moses, taking place shortly after their departure from Sinai (Num. 12:1), would have most likely occurred shortly after her arrival to camp as revealed in Exodos 18.

⁸ And Moses told his father in law all that the LORD had done unto Pharaoh and to the Egyptians for Israel's sake, *and* **all the travail that had come upon them by the way, and** *how* **the LORD delivered them. ⁹ And Jethro rejoiced for all the goodness which the LORD had done to Israel, whom he had delivered out of the hand of the Egyptians. ¹⁰ And Jethro said, Blessed** *be* **the LORD, who hath delivered you out of the hand of the Egyptians, and out of the hand of Pharaoh, who hath delivered the people from under the hand of the Egyptians. ¹¹ Now I know that the LORD is greater than all gods: for in the thing wherein they dealt proudly** *he was* **above them.**

Now I know that the Lord is greater than all gods: this does not lend toward a declaration of monotheistic faith by Jethro but is perhaps best explained by what is considered monolatry, a Greek term that expresses *the exclusive obeisance and recognition to one deity while excluding all others*. Jethro's veneration of Israel's God captures the fulfilment of God's repeated intention; that His supremacy and power would be known in Egypt and beyond. It is interesting that, while Jethro is convinced of Yahweh's powerful intervention, the nation of Israel is not.

[12] And Jethro, Moses' father in law, took a burnt offering and sacrifices for God: and Aaron came, and all the elders of Israel, to eat bread with Moses' father in law before Go [13] And it came to pass on the morrow, that Moses sat to judge the people: and the people stood by Moses from the morning unto the evening. [14] And when Moses' father in law saw all that he did to the people, he said, What is this thing that thou doest to the people? why sittest thou thyself alone, and all the people stand by thee from morning unto even? [15] And Moses said unto his father in law, Because the people come unto me to enquire of God: [16] When they have a matter, they come unto me; and I judge between one and another, and I do make *them* know the statutes of God, and his laws.

I do make them know the statutes of God, and his laws: again, the chronology of Jethro's visit does not seem to coincide with the known events of Exodus. The **statutes of God, and his laws** were not known until Israel had been encamped at Sinai in the third month (Ex. 19:1; 20:1).

[17] And Moses' father in law said unto him, The thing that thou doest is not good. [18] Thou wilt surely wear

away, both thou, and this people that *is* with thee: for this thing *is* too heavy for thee; thou art not able to perform it thyself alone. [19] Hearken now unto my voice, I will give thee counsel, and God shall be with thee: Be thou for the people to God-ward, that thou mayest bring the causes unto God: [20] And thou shalt teach them ordinances and laws, and shalt shew them the way wherein they must walk, and the work that they must do. [21] Moreover thou shalt provide out of all the people able men, such as fear God, men of truth, hating covetousness; and place *such* over them, *to be* rulers of thousands, *and* rulers of hundreds, rulers of fifties, and rulers of tens: [22] And let them judge the people at all seasons: and it shall be, *that* every great matter they shall bring unto thee, but every small matter they shall judge: so shall it be easier for thyself, and they shall bear *the burden* with thee. [23] If thou shalt do this thing, and God command thee so, then thou shalt be able to endure, and all this people shall also go to their place in peace.

Hearken now unto my voice: Jethro's advice to Moses to appoint **able men, such as fear God** that were **men of truth**, hating covetousness reveals the wisdom of his council. Such qualities were to ensure that righteous judgment was administered and that there remained a judicial chain of command. Most importantly, this appointment of judges and rulers would ensure that Moses remained **God-ward** (lit. **before God**). The primary objective of Moses, more than just delivering the people, was to serve as a mediator between Israel and God. Moreover, beyond the mere agency of mediation, Moses would be needed to **teach** (lit. *to shine; send out light*) **the ordinances and laws** concerning their walk and their work (cf. Acts 6:1-4).

²⁴ So Moses hearkened to the voice of his father in law, and did all that he had said. ²⁵ And Moses chose able men out of all Israel, and made them heads over the people, rulers of thousands, rulers of hundreds, rulers of fifties, and rulers of tens. ²⁶ And they judged the people at all seasons: the hard causes they brought unto Moses, but every small matter they judged themselves. ²⁷ And Moses let his father in law depart; and he went his way into his own land.

Made them heads over the people, rulers of thousands: ironically, the very thing the Hebrew slave had resisted after Moses had intervened in the quarrel occurring in Egypt (Ex. 2:14) was now being instituted due to the advice of Jethro.

Notes

CHAPTER 19

¹ In the third month, when the children of Israel were gone forth out of the land of Egypt, the same day came they *into* the wilderness of Sinai.

In the third month: having left Egypt on the 15th day of the first month, this would have placed them arriving at Sinai 45 days later. These figures are of great importance since, on the 46th day, God would call Moses to the top of the mountain and give instructions for the people to purify themselves for three days in preparation for the glory of God that would fall upon the mountain. Exactly 50 days from the Passover in Egypt, the glory of God fell upon the mountain. This event would foreshadow the New Testament events of Pentecost where the Spirit of God fell upon those in the upper room exactly 50 days after the Passover (Acts 2:1-4). The writer of Hebrews would later contrast this event with mount Sion, the heavenly Jerusalem, speaking of the supernatural Kingdom of God realized through the new birth experience as seen in Acts 2:1-4 (Heb. 12:18-22).

² For they were departed from Rephidim, and were come *to* the desert of Sinai, and had pitched in the wilderness;

and there Israel camped before the mount. ³ And Moses went up unto God, and the LORD called unto him out of the mountain, saying, Thus shalt thou say to the house of Jacob, and tell the children of Israel; ⁴ Ye have seen what I did unto the Egyptians, and *how* I bare you on eagles' wings, and brought you unto myself.

Moses went up unto God: it is assumed that Moses returned to the place that God had first spoken to him from the burning bush, perhaps remembering the former promise of God that, after bringing the people out of Egypt he would serve God upon the mountain (Ex. 3:12). However, instead of speaking to Moses from the bush God **called** him from **the mountain**.

Thus shalt thou say to the house of Jacob: this is the second time that the house of Jacob is mentioned. The first occurs upon the arrival of Jacob's small household into Egypt (Gen. 46:27) whereas, in this instance, it is the arrival of the multiplied and prosperous household of Jacob at the foot of Sinai.

⁵ Now therefore, if ye will obey my voice indeed, and keep my covenant, then ye shall be a peculiar treasure unto me above all people: for all the earth is mine: ⁶ And ye shall be unto me a kingdom of priests, and an holy nation. These *are* the words which thou shalt speak unto the children of Israel.

Ye shall be a peculiar treasure: the conditional promise of God to those whom He had borne **on eagle's wings** (cf. Deut. 32:11) was that they would become to God a **peculiar treasure** סְגֻלָּה (*segullāh*), a unique Hebrew word that is difficult to translate, yet whose meaning implies an *exclusive ownership of something holding* *tremendous value.* (cf. Deut. 7:6; 14:2; 26:18; Ps. 135:4). It is important to note, that the language carries a strong matrimonial emphasis that far exceeds the standard Suzerain Treaties (covenant agreements between feudal overlords and submitted vassals) that were prevalent during this time.

A kingdom of priests, and an holy nation: They were to be a **kingdom of priests** (cf. Rev. 1:6); a mediatory **holy nation**, commissioned and set apart to act as God's agency in the world to reveal the character and attributes of the One True God. The covenant between Israel and God was to be one of monogamy and monotheism, an exclusive, dedicated, and undivided relationship that bore responsibilities, both of holiness and of service. In the New Testament, I Peter 2:9 quotes directly from this passage of scripture and parallels the church whose purpose was to *shew forth the praises of God.*

⁷ And Moses came and called for the elders of the people, and laid before their faces all these words which the LORD commanded him. ⁸ And all the people answered together, and said, All that the LORD hath spoken we will do. And Moses returned the words of the people unto the LORD.

All that the Lord hath spoken we will do: at first glance, one misses the weight of the people's agreement. This was not merely an affirmation, but rather, it was a ratified covenant between God and the children of Israel. The events to follow would serve as the ceremony that would set the tone for the gravity of the peoples expressed commitment of exclusive service to God.

⁹ And the LORD said unto Moses, Lo, I come unto thee in a thick cloud, that the people may hear when I speak with thee, and believe thee for ever. And Moses told the words of the people unto the LORD. ¹⁰ And the LORD said unto Moses, Go unto the people, and sanctify them to day and to morrow, and let them wash their clothes, ¹¹ And be ready against the third day: for the third day the LORD will come down in the sight of all the people upon mount Sinai.

That the people may hear when I speak: until this point, the children of Israel had merely seen the activity of Moses and the glory of God within the cloud. In this instance, the people would hear, for the first time, the voice of God speaking to Moses. This event, per God's plans, would establish in the mind of the people that Moses did indeed speak with God.

Sanctify them....let them wash their clothes: the three-day process of purification involved strict separation from impurities, abstinence from sexual intercourse (v.15), and the requirement of washing their clothing. The act of washing and the changing of garments is found throughout scripture to often signify a new beginning, such as Jacob's family and their return to Bethel (Gen. 35:2). Again, in the events of Joseph leaving prison and appearing before Pharaoh, the act of washing and changing of garments is recorded (Gen. 41:14). Other examples clearly indicate the symbolism of the action (cf. Lev. 14:8-9, II Sam. 12:20). Incidentally, when Moses had first approached God in the burning bush, he had been required to remove his shoes. In the New Testament, the motif of washing and cleansing is much a part of the born-again experience and covenant relationship with Jesus Christ (I Jn. 1:9; II Cor. 7:1).

12 And thou shalt set bounds unto the people round about, saying, Take heed to yourselves, *that ye* go *not* up into the mount, or touch the border of it: whosoever toucheth the mount shall be surely put to death: 13 There shall not an hand touch it, but he shall surely be stoned, or shot through; whether *it be* beast or man, it shall not live: when the trumpet soundeth long, they shall come up to the mount.

Thou shalt set bounds unto the people round about: it is unclear if Moses established a physical boundary around the people. However, the implied meaning may have only served to reveal that Moses expressed grave limitations on the peoples' approach to the mountain, explaining to them that, anyone who thought to ascend the mountain, man or beast, would die. Also, the strict limitations placed upon approaching the glory of God would serve to instill in the minds of the Israelites the unique position Moses had as their leader since ascension up the mountain was by invitation alone. Unfortunately, later issues with leadership voiced by Aaron and Miriam would fail to remember this important fact (Num. 12:1-8).

14 And Moses went down from the mount unto the people, and sanctified the people; and they washed their clothes. 15 And he said unto the people, Be ready against the third day: come not at *your* wives. 16 And it came to pass on the third day in the morning, that there were thunders and lightnings, and a thick cloud upon the mount, and the voice of the trumpet exceeding loud; so that all the people that *was* in the camp trembled. 17 And Moses brought forth the people out of the camp to meet with God; and they stood at the nether part of the mount. 18 And mount Sinai was altogether on a smoke,

because the LORD descended upon it in fire: and the smoke thereof ascended as the smoke of a furnace, and the whole mount quaked greatly. [19] And when the voice of the trumpet sounded long, and waxed louder and louder, Moses spake, and God answered him by a voice. [20] And the LORD came down upon mount Sinai, on the top of the mount: and the LORD called Moses *up* to the top of the mount; and Moses went up.

Mount Sinai was altogether on a smoke: The writer of Hebrews would later parallel the events at Sinai with the events at Jerusalem's Pentecost declaring, *"For ye are not come unto the mount that might be touched, and that burned with fire, nor unto blackness, and darkness, and tempest"* (Heb. 12:18), signaling for the New Testament believer the transition that had occurred between law and grace.

[21] And the LORD said unto Moses, Go down, charge the people, lest they break through unto the LORD to gaze, and many of them perish. [22] And let the priests also, which come near to the LORD, sanctify themselves, lest the LORD break forth upon them. [23] And Moses said unto the LORD, The people cannot come up to mount Sinai: for thou chargedst us, saying, Set bounds about the mount, and sanctify it. [24] And the LORD said unto him, Away, get thee down, and thou shalt come up, thou, and Aaron with thee: but let not the priests and the people break through to come up unto the LORD, lest he break forth upon them. [25] So Moses went down unto the people, and spake unto them.

Go down, charge the people, lest they break through: Moses expresses confusion at this reiterated commandment of God since God had already specified borders around the mountain and fatal consequences for anyone that approached. There is perhaps implied here the understanding that many of the children of Israel had not observed the process of sanctification with adequate sobriety. The mention of the **priests**, since the priesthood had yet to be established, may specify the firstborns that had been set apart unto the Lord prior.

So Moses went down: mention of Moses' return with Aaron up the mountain is not revealed. However, as one transitions to the following chapter, Moses has returned and God will relay the laws and statutes that will govern the nation of Israel.

Notes

CHAPTER 20

[1] **And God spake all these words, saying,**

And God spake all these words: here, the very theme and apex of the Exodus story is reached as God delivers what is commonly referred to as the Ten Commandments. A more accurate translation among Hebraic commentary of the Ten Commandments (Decalogue) is known as the *Ten Words*. The law, not just the Ten Words, consisted of three parts: the Decalogue (Ex. 20:1-21), **Civil and Religious Ordinances** (Ex. 20:22-24:11), and **Ceremonial Regulations** (Ex. 24:12-31:18).

The Decalogue, though it's legal structure was not unique to Israel, would emphasize the transcendence and exclusivity of YHWH, thus serving as a foundation for the development and evolution of Israel as a recognized Monotheistic nation. Here, at Sinai, a spiritual revolution within the world would occur. God would begin to establish His identity among His people. Each expressed saying of God would hammer down the revelation of His being. In contrast to other gods of pagan nations, He was outside of nature, time, and space. He was transcendent of all, sustained by none, and without beginning nor end.

Within the Ten Commandments, ritual is absent and a call to both God and man is given an emphasis within a construct of moral and ethical expectations God had for His exclusively possessed, set-apart nation. However, it should be noted that these sayings and commandments cannot be divorced from the narrative of God's intentions for the people. The stipulation of Israel becoming a kingdom of priests, a holy nation, and a peculiar people rested upon their adherence and obedience to the covenantal guidelines established and governed by the Decalogue.

² I *am* the LORD thy God, which have brought thee out of the land of Egypt, out of the house of bondage. ³ Thou shalt have no other gods before me.

I am the Lord thy God: in language similar to the announcements of ancient kings, God expresses his identity in relation to His people. Here, there is a demand for absolute and singular obeisance in **thou shalt have no other gods before me**. This is more than simply the prohibition of *other gods*, but rather, the underlying idea that the concept of other gods is a perverse and corrupted ideology and thus, *other gods should be viewed as non-gods*. This does not refute the knowledge of pagan cultures recognizing and paying homage to false gods, but instead, it establishes in the mind of the Israelites that there are no other true gods. *Yahweh is the only true God* (cf. Jer. 10:10; Jn. 17:3; I Th. 1:9; I Jn. 5:20). This theme of absolute monotheism is consistently reiterated throughout scripture, especially among the prophets who reserve a great deal of emphasis upon the exclusivity of God as a singular, undivided entity that is without equal, who has no co-existing persona, and no comparable likeness (cf. Deut.

6:4; Isa. 40:18; 45:5-6). The devotion of Israel to Yahweh was to reflect the monotheistic nature of God in a way that held to a strict, covenantal monogamy which refused to associate or place any **other gods before** (lit. *in the face of*) Yahweh.

⁴ Thou shalt not make unto thee any graven image, or any likeness of *any thing* that is in heaven above, or that is in the earth beneath, or that is in the water under the earth: ⁵ Thou shalt not bow down thyself to them, nor serve them: for I the LORD thy God am a jealous God, visiting the iniquity of the fathers upon the children unto the third and fourth *generation* of them that hate me; ⁶ And shewing mercy unto thousands of them that love me, and keep my commandments.

Thou shalt not make unto thee any graven image: Building upon the first saying, God recognizes the propensity of humanity to build and hallow the physical to identify and envision the spiritual. The specific prohibition of Israel to develop, shape, or form images, either in likeness or similitude, for the expressed purpose of devotion or worship was underpinned by the monogamous idea of God's jealousy.
This prohibition underscores the error of saint veneration, iconoclastic observance, and religious imagery since it is a gross violation of the monogamous and monotheistic expectations laid out by God for His people.

Further, God would place three restrictions as it related to graven images. First, they were forbidden to make any graven image. Second, they were forbidden to bow down to any graven image. Third, they were forbidden to serve any graven image. Clearly, knowing that man would serve what he worshipped, God erected guidelines that would function as deterrents to avoid this idolatrous outcome. Also, the threefold mention of the realms, (**heavens above, earth below, waters beneath the earth**), encompasses the entirety of the world as it was created in the narrative of Genesis 1 & 2. God was clearly indicating unique singularity of power and authority over all creation (cf. Phi. 2:10; Col. 1:16; Isa. 45:6).

Visiting the iniquities of the fathers upon the children.... mercy unto thousands: the twofold promise of God (visiting iniquities and mercy) are shadows of the stipulated blessing and cursing of God's covenantal relationship with Israel (Lev. 26:3-33). Both responses to God's covenant (obedience or disobedience) carry a long-term, generational impact upon the nation of Israel.

7 Thou shalt not take the name of the LORD thy God in vain; for the LORD will not hold him guiltless that taketh his name in vain.

Thou shalt not take the name of the Lord in vain: commonly misinterpreted to only mean the frivolous articulation of God's name, God prohibits that they should take אָשָׂא (*nāśā'*), meaning *to lift or to carry*, the name of the Lord in vain שָׁוְא (*šāw'*), meaning *empty or worthless*. This commandment expressed a two-fold intention. First, the people of God were to never utilize the name of God in a frivolous and worthless manner. This included, but was not limited to, the practise of cultic sorcery and use of deity's names, as well as, the giving of oaths (Lev. 19:12). Secondly, as the people of the name, they were to live with reverence and sobriety under the expectations the name signified. They were prohibited to *lift up and carry* the name of God while living a lifestyle contrary and opposite of the moral and ethical expectations of God which would result in an empty form of Godliness (cf. II Tim. 3:5).

⁸ Remember the sabbath day, to keep it holy. ⁹ Six days shalt thou labour, and do all thy work: ¹⁰ But the seventh day is the sabbath of the LORD thy God: *in it* thou shalt not do any work, thou, nor thy son, nor thy daughter, thy manservant, nor thy maidservant, nor thy cattle, nor thy stranger that is within thy gates: ¹¹ For *in* six days the LORD made heaven and earth, the sea, and all that in them is, and rested the seventh day: wherefore the LORD blessed the sabbath day, and hallowed it.

Remember the Sabbath Day, to keep it holy: The Hebrew verb remember, זָכַר (*zakar*) most often refers to something from the past (cf. Deut. 9:7-8; 32:7-8; Ps. 25:6) and, in this instance, points backward to the seventh day of Creation where ***God rested from all his work*** (Gen.2:2). There is no scriptural evidence to indicate that anyone, prior to this specific generation, practiced or observed the Sabbath. The unique correlation between the Sabbath, here mentioned, and the Creation Story indicates a very powerful idea of *beginning*. In a sense, having brought Israel out of Egypt and into covenant relationship, God was creatively establishing a new beginning with a nation that was called to establish a heavenly kingdom on earth. This idea is not far from the New Testament's revelation of those birthed into the Kingdom of God (the Church) where they become *new creatures* (II Cor. 5:17). Future commandments regarding the observation of the Sabbath would tie its reason directly to God's deliverance of Israel from

Egypt (Deut. 5:12-17). Therefore, the Sabbath was a sign of Israel's unique position as being a nation set apart (cf. Ex. 31:13), and it would serve to remind them of their *beginning* when God brought them out of Egypt unto the mountain of God where the covenant of service and relationship was established.

¹² Honour thy father and thy mother: that thy days may be long upon the land which the LORD thy God giveth thee.

Transitioning from Israel's obligation to God, the focus now highlights Israel's obligation to humanity. Beginning in the home, they are to honor father and mother which, according to the Apostle Paul, is the first commandment with promise (Eph. 6:2). Indeed, those who observed this commandment were told that their **days would be long upon the land**. Interestingly, this promise is repeated for those would refrained from taking eggs in the presence of a nesting mother (Deut. 22:6-7). In both instances, the home or the nest, *compassion is seen to overwhelm want or needs*. Truly, to honor and esteem one's parents is to set them up in such a way that they are not lacking in resource, shelter, and provision. This would also ensure, in natural understanding, that a precedent would be set for future generations for the care of the aged.

¹³ Thou shalt not kill.

This is not a prohibition against taking life within the context of war, defence, and extreme cases of conflict. Instead, the most accurate translation of this commandment is **thou shalt not murder** תִּרְצָח (*rāsah*), a purely Hebrew term without a modern linguistic equivalent. This commandment is nothing new, for God had already established the precedent against murder while establishing a new beginning with Noah (Gen. 9:6). While the penalty of capital punishment does not accompany the sixth commandment, scripture is emphatically clear elsewhere of the penalty for murder (cf. Lev. 24:17; Num. 35:16). Herein, the sixth through the ninth commandments seek to establish one's responsibility to his/her neighbour. It is not coincidence that the first murder (Gen. 4) was accompanied by a failure of responsibility toward one's brother (Gen. 4:9). It stands to reason that the only true antidote against offending any of these commandments is love (cf. I Jn. 3:4-12; Matt. 22:37-40).

[14] **Thou shalt not commit adultery.**

The sanctity of life is here followed by the sanctity of marriage. Uniquely, both the Sabbath and marriage are two institutions that survived the fall and, as such, scripture is adamant about the continual responsibility between husband and wife to adhere to the marital structure of leave, cleave, and become one flesh (Gen. 2:24; cf. Mat. 19:6). The severity of adultery is revealed in its punishment of death for those apprehended as offenders (cf. Lev. 20:10; Deut. 22:22).

[15] **Thou shalt not steal.**

This commandment is not just a prohibition against the covert act of theft. Instead, it encompasses the entirety of claiming, seizing, or possessing what does not rightfully belong to and/or that which has not been granted. At the heart of this commandment is a two-fold understanding. First, one that loves and values his neighbor would never deign to possess or take what belongs to them. Second, the act of theft undermines confidence in God's promise of provision for His covenant people (cf. Deut. 15:6-8; 28:10-12). This prohibition against stealing applies even to the many *gray areas* of modernity that we often turn a blind eye.

16 Thou shalt not bear false witness against thy neighbour.

The adjudication of crimes, grievance, or legal issues within the collective body of Israel required impartial proceedings that were stipulated by witness testimony. This included, but was not limited, to the failure of one to give testimony if he/she saw or heard anything pertinent to the proceedings (Lev. 5:1). If a witness were found to be false, the penalty that he/she had wished upon the perjured would be required of self (Deut. 19:18).

17 Thou shalt not covet thy neighbour's house, thou shalt not covet thy neighbour's wife, nor his manservant, nor his maidservant, nor his ox, nor his ass, nor any thing that is thy neighbour's.

To covet חָמַד (*hāmad*) is to lust with an almost insatiable craving (Deut. 5:21; 7:25; Jos. 7:21). Desire, in and of itself, is an inerrant quality of ***humanity designed by God. However, humanity is meant to possess desire rather than desire possessing them***. Since this commandment follows the prohibition of adultery, it can best be understood to focus on the internal thoughts and yearnings of illicit desire rather than the actions (Matt. 5:28).

¹⁸ And all the people saw the thunderings, and the lightnings, and the noise of the trumpet, and the mountain smoking: and when the people saw *it*, they removed, and stood afar off. ¹⁹ And they said unto Moses, Speak thou with us, and we will hear: but let not God speak with us, lest we die. ²⁰ And Moses said unto the people, Fear not: for God is come to prove you, and that his fear may be before your faces, that ye sin not. ²¹ And the people stood afar off, and Moses drew near unto the thick darkness where God *was*.

Let not God speak with us, lest we die: having seen the awesome display of thunder, smoke, and the noise of the trumpet, the people **removed** (lit. *staggered*) away from the very boundaries God had established prior (Ex. 19:12). The awesome display of revelation was more than they could stand and, upon Moses' return, they petitioned Moses to serve as an intermediary for them so that they would not risk hearing God speak with them, lest they die. Why God would reveal Himself in such a way is explained by Moses in that **God is come to prove you…that ye sin not**.

²² And the LORD said unto Moses, Thus thou shalt say unto the children of Israel, Ye have seen that I have talked with you from heaven. ²³ Ye shall not make with me gods of silver, neither shall ye make unto you gods of gold.

Ye shall not make with me gods: reiterating the second commandment, God goes further by restricting even the attempt to craft their own imaginations of Yahweh's form. Having just heard a voice but seeing no form further establishes God's careful efforts to hinder the people from developing images of veneration.

Interestingly, the sin of the Golden Calf exposes a direct violation of this explicit commandment.

[24] An altar of earth thou shalt make unto me, and shalt sacrifice thereon thy burnt offerings, and thy peace offerings, thy sheep, and thine oxen: in all places where I record my name I will come unto thee, and I will bless thee.

In all places where I record my name: God would not be bound to one spot alone, as seen in the temporary nature of an earthen altar. Furthermore, it would be God that would choose the place He would set down His manifest glory and operate within the context of His people. The **earthen altar** was most likely was formed by heaping earth together, as seen in the intent of Naaman in II Kings 5:17.

[25] And if thou wilt make me an altar of stone, thou shalt not build it of hewn stone: for if thou lift up thy tool upon it, thou hast polluted it. [26] Neither shalt thou go up by steps unto mine altar, that thy nakedness be not discovered thereon.

An altar of stone: in this instance, God established the restriction against hewing stones to build an altar. Deuteronomy 27:6 indicates that these stones were to be *whole stones*, implying the lack of uniformity and masonry. The stones were to be as they were found upon the ground, in their natural and normal state. Any action taken that would alter the natural shape or condition of the stones was to **pollute** the altar, making it void of God's approval. It was to be the sacrifice, not the creative design and craftsmanship of man, that would be the emphasis of the altar. In both instances,

God sought to establish that He was not to be wooed or impressed by man's devices or lavish talent, but rather, desired altars reminiscent of the Patriarch's.

Neither shalt thou go up by steps: scholars have long been puzzled by this restriction since the priests would later be commanded to wear undergarments to cover their nakedness while ascending the altar associated with the Tabernacle (Ex. 28:42). Because of this, the intention of this commandment may have been for the future building of altars not associated with the priestly service, but instead, altars erected by family elders and leaders. Also, steps would have involved the activity of hewing, which was strictly forbidden on altars of stone. While it seems that steps or a ramp would have been utilized in the future altar built by Solomon, being 10 cubits high (II Chron. 4:1), the brazen altar of the Tabernacle would not have required steps since it was only 3 cubits in height (Ex. 27:1). Perhaps, at least prior to the building of the Temple (which the presence of steps is speculative at the least), God sought to prohibit the wanton practice associated with pagan worship in which elaborate steps and immodest dress was on display for all to see. Some scholars have attempted to explain the nakedness of this passage by utilizing the motif of shame that originates from man's fallen condition (cf. Rev. 3:18).

Notes

CHAPTER 21

The collection of laws found in chapters 22:22-23 are commonly called the **Book of the Covenant** (Ex. 24:7). Chapters 21-22 are written casuistically (in hypothetical cases) such as, *"if thou buy a Hebrew servant..."*, while chapter 23 utilizes the authoritative language similar to the Decalogue's *"thou shalt not."* Aside from the laws found in the Book of the Covenant, there are other legal codes found in the Torah. In Leviticus chapters 17-26, a **code of holiness** is outlined that articulates the laws governing the holiness God expected from His chosen people. Also, in Deuteronomy chapters 12-28 detailed, *specific laws* (expanding upon requirements and principles of chapters 5-11) are given. Many of the laws, regulations, and codes found in these three codes of law were mirrored, in some fashion, within the context of Ancient Near-Eastern contemporary civilizations (i.e. Code of Hammurabi). Because of this, certain laws found in the Book of the Covenant are based upon the assumption that the children of Israel were already familiar with some of the commonplace laws that governed the then Ancient Near Eastern world.

While these laws could not change the human nature, they could **regulate** the same. Looking forward to the time of the Judges, one recognizes the crucial need for the regulatory guidelines and parameters that were set up in that *"every man did that which was right in his own eyes"* (Jdg. 17:6). This revolution of deliverance and sanctification of God's firstborn (Ex. 4:22) marked a radical moment for the entire world. God would impact the macrocosm by a microcosmic holy nation. Yet, for God to truly have a kingdom of priests, He must have a people governed by a social, moral, and religious code that far transcended the secular restraints of human laws alone.

[1] Now these *are* the judgments which thou shalt set before them. [2] If thou buy an Hebrew servant, six years he shall serve: and in the seventh he shall go out free for nothing. [3] If he came in by himself, he shall go out by himself: if he were married, then his wife shall go out with him. [4] If his master have given him a wife, and she have born him sons or daughters; the wife and her children shall be her master's, and he shall go out by himself. [5] And if the servant shall plainly say, I love my master, my wife, and my children; I will not go out free: [6] Then his master shall bring him unto the judges; he shall also bring him to the door, or unto the door post; and his master shall bore his ear through with an aul; and he shall serve him for ever.

If thou buy an Hebrew servant: here, the contractual servant is in mind, typically due to the inability to pay ones debts. It is important to note, that Israel, as a newly liberated nation, had yet to engage in the practice of taking or utilizing slaves. Because of this, knowing the Mesopotamian concepts of slavery, especially considering the Egyptian forced labor and cruelty against the Hebrew nation, God sought to *regulate* a system of domestic servitude that was a very present reality in the Ancient Near East.

These laws, governing the idea of servitude, sought to restrict and avoid any abuse or malpractice the system had the potential to create. The Hebrew legislation regarding servitude emphasized that each servant was a human being, not property. Within the regulations, it was reiterated that any abusive practices that diminished the servant's rights were not allowed and, if violated, punishable! Even further, it protected those unable to pay off debts, provided for the poor, and maintained limits on the length of required servitude (cf. Lev. 25:35-43). Often, life as a servant could be considered more desirable by the Hebrew servants and, having fulfilled the mandatory years of servitude, many servants would voluntarily decide to remain as servants for life, going through the custom of boring through the ear with a piercing instrument at the doorpost of the master's home, thus binding him in body and person to that house for life (cf. Deut. 15:17).

[7] And if a man sell his daughter to be a maidservant, she shall not go out as the menservants do. [8] If she please not her master, who hath betrothed her to himself, then shall he let her be redeemed: to sell her unto a strange nation he shall have no power, seeing he hath dealt deceitfully with her. [9] And if he have betrothed her unto his son, he shall deal with her after the manner of daughters. [10] If he take him another *wife*; her food, her raiment, and her duty of marriage, shall he not diminish. [11] And if he do not these three unto her, then shall she go out free without money.

If a man sell his daughter: here, the conjugal **maidservant** הָמָא (*āmāh*) is described and was considered to have only occurred in the most extreme cases of poverty when all other options failed the father. These arranged marriages, while foreign to our culture, were a present condition of the day. Though such a custom as unsavoury, God sought to enact conditions that would deter cruel practices and customs that could arise and thus, protect the rights and well-being of the conjugal servant. Unlike the male indentured servant, the maidservant was not allowed to go free after 6 years of labour. However, protections and rights were to be given to the maidservant that ensured lifelong provision and security. If the master of the house did not provide the three essentials (food, raiment, and the duty of marriage) she was able to leave without the requirement of payment or price.

[12] He that smiteth a man, so that he die, shall be surely put to death. [13] And if a man lie not in wait, but God deliver *him* into his hand; then I will appoint thee a place whither he shall flee.

In contrast to Hammurabi's Law, which specified a monetary compensation for murders, the Book of the Covenant expresses *life-for-life*, further established by Numbers 35:30-31 which prohibited monetary payment as a substitution for a murderer's execution. To murder was to violate the ancient law expressed in Gen. 9:6, further established by the sixth commandment of *thou shalt not kill*. In the case of accidental murder, God would appoint a place for the offender to flee and obtain fair trial, alluding to the establishment of the Cities of Refuge later appointed after entering the Promise Land (cf. Num. 35:6-24; Deut. 19:1-13; Josh. 20). The asylum alluded to, crossed into the phenomenon of blood feud where, without a centralized judicial government, kinship maintained the right of the *gō ēl hadām* , translated as the "*Avenger of Blood*" (Deut. 19:6, 12: Josh. 20:3,5,9). This allusion to the Laws of Asylum would set into motion the gradual departure from this prevalent custom, later establishing that vengeance belonged to God alone (Lev. 19:18; cf. Rom. 12:19; Heb. 10:30).

[14] But if a man come presumptuously upon his neighbour, to slay him with guile; thou shalt take him from mine altar, that he may die.

We are given here the origin of the actions of two men in scripture, Adonijah and Joab, when they fled to the altar and grasped the altar's horns; an action of desperation that begged for mercy due to crimes of presumptuous slayings (I Kg. 1:50-53; 2:28-34). In both instances, one in the instant and the other occurring later, each man was unable to maintain or defend innocence of their motives and intents.

[15] And he that smiteth his father, or his mother, shall be surely put to death. [16] And he that stealeth a man, and selleth him, or if he be found in his hand, he shall surely be put to death. [17] And he that curseth his father, or his mother, shall surely be put to death.

The capital crimes punishable by death are as follows:

1. Premediated murder (v. 12)

2. Kidnapping (v. 16)

3. Physical violence against parents (v. 15)

4. Cursing of parents (v. 17)

Two of the four capital crimes revolve around the family unit, indicating the importance God gave the sanctity and order of the home. It is important to note that the cursing of one's parents exceeds the mere act of verbal slander, but instead, expresses the idea of a child treating his parents with the utmost contempt. Deuteronomy 21:18-21 provides an in-depth glimpse into the characteristics and behaviors of a child that falls under this category.

[18] And if men strive together, and one smite another with a stone, or with *his* fist, and he die not, but keepeth *his* bed: [19] If he rise again, and walk abroad upon his staff, then shall he that smote *him* be quit: only he shall pay *for* the loss of his time, and shall cause *him* to be thoroughly healed. [20] And if a man smite his servant, or his maid, with a rod, and he die under his hand; he shall be surely punished. [21] Notwithstanding, if he continue a day or two, he shall not be punished: for he is his money.

If a man smite his servant, or his maid...: If not careful, these scriptures can be viewed anachronistically by imposing modern culture into Near Eastern antiquity. Clearly, within the societal norms at the time of Israel's formation, corporal punishment was an established part of society, as it remains among many modern cultures even today. Once again, it is important to understand that these times lacked what we call a "middle class." Slavery, as seen in scripture, typically resulted in the voluntary indenture of one seeking to pay off a debt or one living in poverty who needed shelter, food, and clothing. The "life for life", in the case of premediated murder, still applied to the master/servant relationship. We see also, based upon **21:26-27**, that physical damage to a servant by one's master demanded the servant be set free. While these laws often produce tension for the modern reader, it is important to understand that God was establishing checks and balances far exceeding the cultural norms prevalent among contemporary civilizations.

22 If men strive, and hurt a woman with child, so that her fruit depart *from her***, and yet no mischief follow: he shall be surely punished, according as the woman's husband will lay upon him; and he shall pay as the judges** *determine.* **23 And if** *any* **mischief follow, then thou shalt give life for life, 24 Eye for eye, tooth for tooth, hand for hand, foot for foot, 25 Burning for burning, wound for wound, stripe for stripe.**

Eye for an eye, tooth for tooth: The law of retaliation (Lat. *Lex Talionus*) in the Bible often expressed as an *eye for an eye* is not unique to the Torah law. It was clearly reflected in the various laws and codes of Mesopotamian legal society. Scripture, differing from many of the contemporary legal codes, sought to enforce equal justice that was not influenced by one's socioeconomic status.

26 And if a man smite the eye of his servant, or the eye of his maid, that it perish; he shall let him go free for his eye's sake. 27 And if he smite out his manservant's tooth, or his maidservant's tooth; he shall let him go free for his tooth's sake. 28 If an ox gore a man or a woman, that they die: then the ox shall be surely stoned, and his flesh shall not be eaten; but the owner of the ox *shall* **be quit. 29 But if the ox were wont to push with his horn in time past, and it hath been testified to his owner, and he hath not kept him in, but that he hath killed a man or a woman; the ox shall be stoned, and his owner also shall**

be put to death. ³⁰ If there be laid on him a sum of money, then he shall give for the ransom of his life whatsoever is laid upon him. ³¹ Whether he have gored a son, or have gored a daughter, according to this judgment shall it be done unto him. ³² If the ox shall push a manservant or a maidservant; he shall give unto their master thirty shekels of silver, and the ox shall be stoned.

If the ox were wont to push with his horn: here scripture indicates an ox with an aggressive nature that has attempted to, or succeeded in, goring other human beings though not resulting in death. If the owner of the ox did not take the proper precautions (tying the ox or cutting its horns) and the ox killed a human being, life for life applied (Gen. 9:5-6). This provision removed any attempts at the owner of the ox to avoid blame though provision was made for a ransom of thirty shekels and the subsequent stoning of the ox.

³³ And if a man shall open a pit, or if a man shall dig a pit, and not cover it, and an ox or an ass fall therein; ³⁴ The owner of the pit shall make *it* good, *and* give money unto the owner of them; and the dead *beast* shall be his. ³⁵ And if one man's ox hurt another's, that he die; then they shall sell the live ox, and divide the money of it; and the dead ox also they shall divide. ³⁶ Or if it be known that the ox hath used to push in time past, and his owner hath not kept him in; he shall surely pay ox for ox; and the dead shall be his own.

Notes

CHAPTER 22

¹ If a man shall steal an ox, or a sheep, and kill it, or sell it; he shall restore five oxen for an ox, and four sheep for a sheep. ² If a thief be found breaking up, and be smitten that he die, *there shall* no blood *be shed* for him. ³ If the sun be risen upon him, there *shall be* blood *shed* for him; *for* he should make full restitution; if he have nothing, then he shall be sold for his theft. ⁴ If the theft be certainly found in his hand alive, whether it be ox, or ass, or sheep; he shall restore double.

If a man shall steal: many of the legislative codes of contemporary nations decreed the death of one found guilty of theft. Here, God's legislation promotes a degree of compassion that sought to preserve and maintain the sanctity of life. Physical property, though valued, could not justify the death of a human being. However, if the thief was killed while breaking in under the obscurity of night (Job 24:16), the homeowner would not be held to life-for-life under the provision that he could not know the intentions or purpose of the one breaking in. However, a reversal of this would apply if the theft were to occur in daylight. Obviously, though the thief was in the wrong, human property still could not take precedent over human life and, if the owner were not in danger of life and killed the thief, bloodguilt would apply. Modern cultures still reflect many of these fundamental provisions enacted against household theft.

⁵ If a man shall cause a field or vineyard to be eaten, and shall put in his beast, and shall feed in another man's field; of the best of his own field, and of the best of his own vineyard, shall he make restitution. ⁶ If fire break out, and catch in thorns, so that the stacks of corn, or the standing corn, or the field, be consumed *therewith*; he that kindled the fire shall surely make restitution.

⁷ If a man shall deliver unto his neighbour money or stuff to keep, and it be stolen out of the man's house; if the thief be found, let him pay double. ⁸ If the thief be not found, then the master of the house shall be brought unto the judges, to see whether he have put his hand unto his neighbour's goods. ⁹ For all manner of trespass, *whether it be* for ox, for ass, for sheep, for raiment, or for any manner of lost thing, which *another* challengeth to be his, the cause of both parties shall come before the judges; *and* whom the judges shall condemn, he shall pay double unto his neighbour. ¹⁰ If a man deliver unto his neighbour an ass, or an ox, or a sheep, or any beast, to keep; and it die, or be hurt, or driven away, no man seeing it: ¹¹ *Then* shall an oath of the LORD be between them both, that he hath not put his hand unto his neighbour's goods; and the owner of it shall accept *thereof*, and he shall not make it good. ¹² And if it be stolen from him, he shall make restitution unto the owner thereof. ¹³ If it be torn in pieces, *then* let him bring it *for* witness, *and* he shall not make good that which was torn. ¹⁴ And if a man borrow *ought* of his neighbour, and it be hurt, or die, the owner thereof being not with it, he shall surely make it

good. ¹⁵ *But* if the owner thereof *be* with it, he shall not make *it* good: if it *be* an hired *thing*, it came for his hire.

22:7:15: These verses highlight the relationship between bailer/bailee and the custody of goods (ox, ass, sheep, raiment, and other properties). The burden of responsibility, as it should be, would lie with the borrower and thus, the burden of proof to dispute any degree of negligence that resulted of loss, harm, or disappearance also lay with the borrower. Such proof was to be sought *before the Lord*, implying the grave position of one swearing under oath with the Lord as witness. Fundamentally, these laws sought to avoid violence, strife, and harm between the bailer and bailee, thus ensuring that the proper relationship with one's neighbor was maintained. Many of these principles are apropos within the Kingdom of God today, where too many instances of relational damage have occurred due to ownership, property, and materials.

¹⁶ And if a man entice a maid that is not betrothed, and lie with her, he shall surely endow her to be his wife. ¹⁷ If her father utterly refuse to give her unto him, he shall pay money according to the dowry of virgins.

If a man entice a maid that is not betrothed: a more detailed list of laws is laid out in Deuteronomy 22:23-29 indicating that this particular law, as it is found within the context of other laws, was not meant to be exhaustive. The father, as custodian of his daughter, would have legal recourse to ensure that his daughter was taken care of if she were **enticed** (lit. *seduced*). Since the customs of virgin betrothal were different than they are in many cases today, this law afforded protections that would prohibit the negligence of the said men from and ensuring they care for the women, and perhaps the children, that occurred after sexual activity.

¹⁸ Thou shalt not suffer a witch to live.

This is the first of three series of statutes against various idolatrous customs that were punishable by death. Scripture is very clear as to the ***abomination*** of those who practice the various arts of witchcraft (cf. Deut. 18:9-14). The prevalence of such detestable arts has always been an integral part of pagan cultures, even finding its way into the New Testament as an opponent to the Apostles during their missionary journeys (Acts 13:6-11). The practice of ***all magic***, not just those considered evil and/or destructive, was forbidden. Any magic, even those which claim to benefit life and health, was forbidden and punishable by death. A unique difference is noted here as to the penalty of sorcery. Whereas other capital crimes often utilize the phrase ***put to death***, here the phrase is literally, ***not let live***. In other words, while the penalty was indeed death, scripture makes an emphasis against the Israelites **tolerating** the practice of divination or sorcery in their midst. This strict prohibition and the clear abhorrence of God against its practice should be considered in lieu of a society that now celebrates (even glorifies) many of the ideas and concepts found in sorcery and witchcraft.

¹⁹ Whosoever lieth with a beast shall surely be put to death.

Bestiality was often associated with sorcerous practices and sometimes customary among the idolatrous rituals of pagan cultures. Pagan mythology is rife with instances of sexual interaction between gods and animals, often to divert calamity or to secure healing from terrible plights. Obviously, the influence of such practices, as well as the unrestrained flesh of humanity, led to a strict prohibition and the punishment of death if one were to be found guilty of such an abhorrent act (cf. Lev. 22:16; 28:23; Deut. 27:21).

[20] He that sacrificeth unto *any* god, save unto the LORD only, he shall be utterly destroyed. [21] Thou shalt neither vex a stranger, nor oppress him: for ye were strangers in the land of Egypt.

Thou shalt neither vex a stranger: the linking reason, for ye were strangers in Egypt, underscores the transcendence of God's Kingdom within the Earth. Lest Israel adopt the same tyrannical nature of the Egyptians where oppression and cruelty was exercised simply because the Israelites were an alien nation, God sought to keep Israel's bondage in remembrance. God knew that once one suppresses the basic human rights of another, regardless of national origin, the doors to such practices would be opened.

[22] Ye shall not afflict any widow, or fatherless child. [23] If thou afflict them in any wise, and they cry at all unto me, I will surely hear their cry; [24] And my wrath shall wax hot, and I will kill you with the sword; and your wives shall be widows, and your children fatherless.

A strong emphasis is placed upon a protection of the needy and poor, the orphans and the widows and any potential oppression against the sojourner. The concern for such individuals was not merely a humanitarian expectation but a divine decree. Failure to adhere to these expectations constituted a grievous sin that carried with it generation ramifications. Sadly, Israel would find itself as the object of prophetic rebuke for their continual failure to care for and not oppress the disadvantaged of society (cf. Ezek. 22:7, 29). Weakness has long been exploited by society and, because of this, God sought to underscore the responsibility of His people to reflect the nature of compassion, as found in the future example of Jesus Christ.

25 If thou lend money to *any* of my people *that is* poor by thee, thou shalt not be to him as an usurer, neither shalt thou lay upon him usury. 26 If thou at all take thy neighbour's raiment to pledge, thou shalt deliver it unto him by that the sun goeth down: 27 For that is his covering only, it is his raiment for his skin: wherein shall he sleep? and it shall come to pass, when he crieth unto me, that I will hear; for I *am* gracious.

Niether shalt thou lay upon him usury: the word **usury** נֶשֶׁךְ (*neshek*) comes from the Hebrew word נָשַׁךְ (*nashak*) which means *"to bite"*. This is a clear allusion to the strike of **serpent** נָחָשׁ (*nachash*) lending toward the venomous viewpoint God has toward charging interest against a fellow brothers loan, especially when he is already poor and merely seeking to rectify his position in life (cf. Ps. 15:5; Prov. 28:8; Ezek. 18:8, 13, 17; 22:12). God sought to once again underscore that even the practice of lending was to be undergird by compassion since nothing was outside of the watchful attention of God (Deut. 24:12-13).

28 Thou shalt not revile the gods, nor curse the ruler of thy people.

Israel was to give reverence toward the **magistrates**

(used here as *gods*, *elohim*, a word often used to signify *judges* in the Old Testament) is expressed (cf. Acts 23:5). Though one may find themselves in dire straits, they must never curse God, nor those who filled the role of magistrate or king (cf. II Sam. 16:13; I Kgs. 21:10; Isa. 8:21).

²⁹ Thou shalt not delay *to offer* **the first of thy ripe fruits, and of thy liquors: the firstborn of thy sons shalt thou give unto me. ³⁰ Likewise shalt thou do with thine oxen,** *and* **with thy sheep: seven days it shall be with his dam; on the eighth day thou shalt give it me. ³¹ And ye shall be holy men unto me: neither shall ye eat** *any* **flesh** *that is* **torn of beasts in the field; ye shall cast it to the dogs.**

Thou shalt not delay the first of thy ripe fruits: the word **delay**, אָחַר (*achar*), typically translates as *tarry*. The practice of *holding back* or *changing the order* of the first fruit may be implied here. Likewise (in the same manner) one was to strictly hold to the specified order of time in which the firstborn of livestock was given to the Lord. Simply put, the first fruit was to be given first! Anything that changed this order negated the power of the first and the implications of its designation (cf. Prov. 3:9).

Notes

CHAPTER 23

¹ Thou shalt not raise a false report: put not thine hand with the wicked to be an unrighteous witness. ² Thou shalt not follow a multitude to *do* evil; neither shalt thou speak in a cause to decline after many to wrest *judgment*: ³ Neither shalt thou countenance a poor man in his cause.

Neither shalt thou countenance a poor man in his cause: one must never allow class, rich or poor, to affect righteous judgment (cf. Lev. 19:15). Justice is to be blind to the status or lack thereof when it comes to righteous judgment. Verse 6 reiterates this further.

⁴ If thou meet thine enemy's ox or his ass going astray, thou shalt surely bring it back to him again. ⁵ If thou see the ass of him that hateth thee lying under his burden, and wouldest forbear to help him, thou shalt surely help with him. ⁶ Thou shalt not wrest the judgment of thy poor in his cause. ⁷ Keep thee far from a false matter; and the innocent and righteous slay thou not: for I will not justify the wicked. ⁸ And thou shalt take no gift: for the gift blindeth the wise, and perverteth the words of the righteous. ⁹ Also thou shalt not oppress a stranger: for ye know the heart of a stranger, seeing ye were strangers in the land of Egypt.

Thou shalt take no gift: that is to say, take nothing that constitutes a bribe. There is no place for the judge to take anything of monetary or sentimental value that could pervert or give the perception of perverting justice (cf. Deut. 16:19).

[10] And six years thou shalt sow thy land, and shalt gather in the fruits thereof: [11] But the seventh *year* thou shalt let it rest and lie still; that the poor of thy people may eat: and what they leave the beasts of the field shall eat. In like manner thou shalt deal with thy vineyard, *and* with thy oliveyard. [12] Six days thou shalt do thy work, and on the seventh day shalt rest: that thine ox and thine ass may rest, and the son of thy handmaid, and the stranger, may be refreshed.

Here, the Agricultural Sabbath following the possession of Canaan (Num. 26) is alluded to. The ***Agricultural Sabbath***, a provision for the poor and the beasts of the field (Ex. 23:11), established several fundamental premises for the nation of Israel. First, it established that the earth is the Lords (Ex. 9:29; Deut. 10:14; Ps. 24:1) and that, as the owner, God had given it to man who would act as a faithful steward (Ps. 115:16). Second, the blessing of the sixth-year harvest (vss. 20-21) established an understanding of the covenantal blessings of God if they were to keep God's judgments and statues (**v. 18**). Third, it also established a healthy cycle for the soil where various processes were allowed to run their course, thus allowing for a renewing of reproduction.

[13] And in all *things* that I have said unto you be circumspect: and make no mention of the name of other gods, neither let it be heard out of thy mouth.

Make no mention of the name of other gods: Israel was to be **circumspect** (lit. *watchful*) of all the things God had commanded them. In this case, they were to take the utmost care to never associate or invoke the pagan gods and idolatry of pagan cultures into the practices and rites of God's sacred seasons and feasts. Quite literally, they were not to *think or speak* of any such things.

¹⁴ Three times thou shalt keep a feast unto me in the year.

Three annual pilgrimage feasts are intended here: The Feast of Unleavened Bread, the Feast of Weeks (Pentecost), and the Feast of Tabernacles.

¹⁵ Thou shalt keep the feast of unleavened bread: (thou shalt eat unleavened bread seven days, as I commanded thee, in the time appointed of the month Abib; for in it thou camest out from Egypt: and none shall appear before me empty:)

On the evening of the Passover, the **feast of unleavened bread** was to be observed for seven days as a reminder of the day Israel came out of Egypt with *great haste* after eating the *bread of affliction* (cf. Deut. 16:3; Ex. 12:39).

¹⁶ And the feast of harvest, the firstfruits of thy labours, which thou hast sown in the field: and the feast of ingathering, *which is* in the end of the year, when thou hast gathered in thy labours out of the field. ¹⁷ Three times in the year all thy males shall appear before the Lord GOD.

The **Feast of Firstfruits**, here called the **feast of harvest**, marked the beginning of the barley-grain harvests that would not be practiced until after Israel entered the Promised Land. Here, the future harvests of Israel would remain unavailable to them until a **sheaf** (meaning, *a measure*) was brought by the priesthood to the house of God where it would then be **waved** (lit. *elevated*) before the Lord in order to gain acceptance. Such an offering was an acknowledgement that the first gleanings of fruit and agriculture belonged to God (Deut. 26:8-10), thereby securing Gods approval and blessing (cf. Ezek. 44:30; Lev. 19:24-25).

The true significance of this feast was that it set into motion what is commonly referred to as the *Counting of the Omer*, which was the fifty-day countdown to the **Feast of Weeks**, commonly referred to as Pentecost. The **Feast of Firstfirsts** was realized in the resurrection of Jesus Christ who became the *firstfruit of the dead* (I Cor. 15:20; Rev. 1:5), pointing toward the harvest that would follow the observance of seven Sabbaths, culminating on the fiftieth-day called Pentecost (Acts. 2:1-4), where those who were *dead in their trespasses* (Eph. 2:1) were resurrected into Christ through the infilling of the Holy Ghost, evidenced by their speaking with other tongues (Acts 2:1-4, Titus 3:5; I Pet. 1:3; Rom. 6:5-10).

The feast of ingathering: to commemorate the 40 years that Israel had lived in tents, the Israelites were to close out the year with the Feast of Tabernacles (Lev. 23).

[18] Thou shalt not offer the blood of my sacrifice with leavened bread; neither shall the fat of my sacrifice remain until the morning. [19] The first of the firstfruits of thy land thou shalt bring into the house of the LORD thy God. Thou shalt not seethe a kid in his mother's milk.

Seeth a kid in his mother's milk: this commandant, appearing here and two other times in scripture (Ex. 34:26; Deut. 14:21), has longed remained an enigma and falls under a category of laws called *hukkim*; laws that have no obvious explanations. Some have proposed that to **seethe** לְשַׁבֵּ, (*bishul*) a kid in its mother's milk may have merely sought to avoid the cruelty while others thought this may have been a Canaanite custom practiced within idolatrous circumstances. Others think that the requirement to keep a kid seven days with its mother is here indirectly implied (Lev. 23:27). Though interpretations vary, restrictions of meat and milk have since broadened to encompass many other animals as a staple kosher restriction among current observant Jews.

[20] Behold, I send an Angel before thee, to keep thee in the way, and to bring thee into the place which I have prepared. [21] Beware of him, and obey his voice, provoke him not; for he will not pardon your transgressions: for my name *is* in him. [22] But if thou shalt indeed obey his voice, and do all that I speak; then I will be an enemy unto thine enemies, and an adversary unto thine adversaries. [23] For mine Angel shall go before thee, and bring thee in unto the Amorites, and the Hittites, and the Perizzites, and the Canaanites, the Hivites, and the Jebusites: and I will cut them off.

Behold I send an angel before you: it should be noted that the idea of the **Angel of the Lord** should not be thought of as a separate entity from God, but rather, *the direction and guidance of God*, either *by will or by manifested agency*, such as, the pillar of cloud *that accompanied Israel on their journey* (cf. Ex. 14;19; Num. 20:16). Similar verbiage is used by Abraham, whereas no separation is made later between the angel of the Lord and God's guidance in the way (cf. Gen. 24:7, 27). Regardless of the manifestation chosen by God to accompany Israel on their journey, God's **name was in him**, which implies the authority of God's directing presence. Similarly, Jesus Christ was come in his Father's name (Jn. 5:43), which is to say, Christ was the visible agency of God's salvation and, to see Christ, one saw the Father (Jn. 14:9). In this instance of wilderness journeying, the agency of God (pillar of cloud or angel of the Lord) served as a utility to manifest God's glory among the people from which God would speak, command, and observe.

24 Thou shalt not bow down to their gods, nor serve them, nor do after their works: but thou shalt utterly overthrow them, and quite break down their images. 25 And ye shall serve the LORD your God, and he shall bless thy bread, and thy water; and I will take sickness away from the midst of thee.

A common consequence of disobedience and idolatry is found in God bringing disease upon lawbreakers (2 Chron. 21:15; Deut. 28:61). Here, the promise of taking away said sickness would be the result of strict adherence to exclusively worship and obey Him.

26 There shall nothing cast their young, nor be barren, in thy land: the number of thy days I will fulfil.

There shall nothing cast their young, nor be barren: the phrase, cast their young, literally implies the tragedy of miscarriage. Miscarriage and barrenness would not be found in the women of Israel. Looking back at the struggle with barrenness by the Matriarchs, one sees the significance of such a promise to the generation called to inherit the promise.

²⁷ I will send my fear before thee, and will destroy all the people to whom thou shalt come, and I will make all thine enemies turn their backs unto thee. ²⁸ And I will send hornets before thee, which shall drive out the Hivite, the Canaanite, and the Hittite, from before thee. ²⁹ I will not drive them out from before thee in one year; lest the land become desolate, and the beast of the field multiply against thee. ³⁰ By little and little I will drive them out from before thee, until thou be increased, and inherit the land.

The sending of hornets likely utilizes the imagery of the insect's relentless aggression and bitter sting, though scripture seems to allude to an agency of aggressive pursuit (Deut. 7:20) and the reason for the Amorite kings being driven out during Joshua's campaign (Josh. 24:12). Interestingly, God's plan involved the gradual driving out of Israel's enemy **little by little** until the Israelites were of a number that they could conquer both the fertilization of the land and the wild beasts of the field. This reveals an intriguing aspect of God's conquest of Canaan; utilizing the enemy to subdue the land's beasts and soil until the strength of the children of God was capable to step in.

³¹ And I will set thy bounds from the Red sea even unto the sea of the Philistines, and from the desert unto the river: for I will deliver the inhabitants of the land into your hand; and thou shalt drive them out before thee. ³² Thou shalt make no covenant with them, nor with their gods. ³³ They shall not dwell in thy land, lest they make thee sin against me: for if thou serve their gods, it will surely be a snare unto thee.

Notes

CHAPTER 24

¹ And he said unto Moses, Come up unto the LORD, thou, and Aaron, Nadab, and Abihu, and seventy of the elders of Israel; and worship ye afar off. ² And Moses alone shall come near the LORD: but they shall not come nigh; neither shall the people go up with him. ³ And Moses came and told the people all the words of the LORD, and all the judgments: and all the people answered with one voice, and said, All the words which the LORD hath said will we do. ⁴ And Moses wrote all the words of the LORD, and rose up early in the morning, and builded an altar under the hill, and twelve pillars, according to the twelve tribes of Israel.

And Moses...builded an altar under the hill: at the foot of Mount Sinai, Moses erected an altar of either earth or unhewn stone (cf. Ex. 20:24) for the future ceremony that would ratify the covenant between God and the people. Opposite the altar, Moses erected twelve pillars that corresponded to the whole congregation of Israel (twelve tribes).

⁵ And he sent young men of the children of Israel, which offered burnt offerings, and sacrificed peace offerings of oxen unto the LORD. ⁶ And Moses took

half of the blood, and put *it* in basons; and half of the blood he sprinkled on the altar. ⁷ And he took the book of the covenant, and read in the audience of the people: and they said, All that the LORD hath said will we do, and be obedient. ⁸ And Moses took the blood, and sprinkled it on the people, and said, Behold the blood of the covenant, which the LORD hath made with you concerning all these words.

Moses took...the blood: blood was often used in the ratification of covenants in the Ancient Near-Eastern cultures. Having the events of the 10th plague still fresh in their minds, the action of sprinkling blood would have carried a tremendous impact upon the people. Blood had already proven a *redemptive agent* in their lives but now it would serve as an *adoptive agent*, bringing them into a covenantal relationship with the One True God.

Moses...sprinkled half the blood: first throwing blood from one basin onto the altar, Moses read again the Book of the Covenant (cf. II Kings 23:2; Neh. 8:5-9) and the people answered in the affirmative that they would fulfil their end of the agreement.

Moses...sprinkling it on the people: More than likely, rather than throwing blood from the other basin toward the physical congregation of Israel, Moses cast the blood upon the twelve stones that represented the nation declaring, **behold the blood of the covenant**, a phrase that foreshadowed the everlasting covenant of blood revealed in the dispensation of grace through the redemptive actions of Jesus Christ and the shedding of His blood at Calvary (cf. Heb. 10:29; 12:24; 13:20).

⁹ Then went up Moses, and Aaron, Nadab, and Abihu, and seventy of the elders of Israel: ¹⁰ And they saw the God of Israel: and *there was* **under his feet as it were a paved work of a sapphire stone, and as it were the body of heaven in** *his* **clearness.**

The image of the seventy elders, along with Moses, Aaron, and his children, parallels several other instances in scripture where a likeness or similitude of God is seen (cf. Ezek. 1:26; Dan. 7:9,13). Nothing is described of the form of God (cf. Num. 12:8), but rather, an emphasis on the medium through which they vaguely perceived whatever form God appeared in. The sapphire stone is also unique to Ezekiel's image of the throne of God (Ezek: 1:26; 10:1) whereas here, it seems to present itself with the essence of the firmament in all its luster. One thinks of the Apostle Paul's imagery of *seeing through a glass darkly* (I Cor. 13:12) and wonders if, in some measure, this was a meager idea of what they viewed.

¹¹ And upon the nobles of the children of Israel he laid not his hand: also they saw God, and did eat and drink.

The unique circumstances of promised safety and blessings for covenantal obedience would be followed by the act of eating and drinking, thus implying a covenantal meal (cf. Gen. 31:46, 54; Ex. 18:12). One sees this mirrored in a greater dimension during the supper between Christ and His disciples (Matt. 26:26-29; Mark 14:22-23; Lk. 22:19-20).

¹² And the LORD said unto Moses, Come up to me into the mount, and be there: and I will give thee tables of stone, and a law, and commandments which I have written; that thou mayest teach them. ¹³ And Moses rose

up, and his minister Joshua: and Moses went up into the mount of God. ¹⁴ And he said unto the elders, Tarry ye here for us, until we come again unto you: and, behold, Aaron and Hur *are* with you: if any man have any matters to do, let him come unto them.

Delegation of authority in Moses' absence is assigned to the seventy elders who, upon any **men having matters to do** (implying legal matters) were to redirect judgment to Aaron and Hur. It needs to be noted that Hur is absent from the account of the Golden Calf.

¹⁵ And Moses went up into the mount, and a cloud covered the mount. ¹⁶ And the glory of the LORD abode upon mount Sinai, and the cloud covered it six days: and the seventh day he called unto Moses out of the midst of the cloud. ¹⁷ And the sight of the glory of the LORD *was* like devouring fire on the top of the mount in the eyes of the children of Israel. ¹⁸ And Moses went into the midst of the cloud, and gat him up into the mount: and Moses was in the mount forty days and forty nights.

Notes

Chapter 25

¹ And the LORD spake unto Moses, saying, ² Speak unto the children of Israel, that they bring me an offering: of every man that giveth it willingly with his heart ye shall take my offering. ³ And this is the offering which ye shall take of them; gold, and silver, and brass, ⁴ And blue, and purple, and scarlet, and fine linen, and goats' *hair*, ⁵ And rams' skins dyed red, and badgers' skins, and shittim wood, ⁶ Oil for the light, spices for anointing oil, and for sweet incense, ⁷ Onyx stones, and stones to be set in the ephod, and in the breastplate. ⁸ And let them make me a sanctuary; that I may dwell among them. ⁹ According to all that I shew thee, *after* the pattern of the tabernacle, and the pattern of all the instruments thereof, even so shall ye make it.

The **Tabernacle** מִשְׁכָּן (*mishkān*) is a masterpiece of Biblical typology, whose construction adheres to a specific **pattern** (lit. form or likeness) which the New Testament reveals was after *the example and shadow of things heavenly* (Heb. 8:5). Every feature and exhibit of the Tabernacle reveals, in type, some aspect of Jesus Christ, and/or the Kingdom of God on Earth as revealed through the New Testament church. As an example and shadow of things heavenly, the Tabernacle pointed prophetically to the work and ministry of Jesus

Christ, the Great High Priest, who would enter into heaven itself (cf. Heb. 9:24), and accomplish the work of redemption through the atoning work secured in the events of Calvary. The functional importance of the Tabernacle, the dwelling of God, would find its earthly realization on the Day of Pentecost (cf. Acts 2) when the Spirit would dwell in temples not made with hands, referring to the lives of New Testament believers (cf. Acts 2:38; I Cor. 3:16; 6:19) a clear fulfillment of Old Testament prophecies (cf. Ezek. 11:19; 36:26; Joel 2:28-29). As the New Testament church, individual believers, though many, are building up together a habitation of God (cf. Eph. 2:22).

¹⁰ And they shall make an ark of shittim wood: two cubits and a half *shall be* **the length thereof, and a cubit and a half the breadth thereof, and a cubit and a half the height thereof. ¹¹ And thou shalt overlay it with pure gold, within and without shalt thou overlay it, and shalt make upon it a crown of gold round about. ¹² And thou shalt cast four rings of gold for it, and put** *them* **in the four corners thereof; and two rings** *shall be* **in the one side of it, and two rings in the other side of it. ¹³ And thou shalt make staves** *of* **shittim wood, and overlay them with gold. ¹⁴ And thou shalt put the staves into the rings by the sides of the ark, that the ark may be borne with them. ¹⁵ The staves shall be in the rings of the ark: they shall not be taken from it. ¹⁶ And thou shalt put into the ark the testimony which I shall give thee.**

Thou shalt make an ark: the word **ark** אֲרוֹן, (*'arôn*) signifies a chest or box that, in this case, was to be made from the wood of acacia trees, overlaid with gold. The Ark of the Covenant, called also the Ark of the Testimony, would house the two tablets of stone called the Ten Commandments, a golden pot of manna, and Aaron's Rod that budded (cf. Heb. 9:4). The Ark of the Covenant was the centerpiece of the Tabernacle that, when carried, was never to be directly touched by human hands (II Sam. 6:6) but borne by the staves thrust through rings. Even during its travels, it was to remain ahead of the congregation of Israel and was always wrapped in the veil, with the covering of badger's skin laid upon it, and a cloth of pure blue laid over the top (cf. Num. 4:5-6).

17 And thou shalt make a mercy seat *of* pure gold: two cubits and a half *shall be* the length thereof, and a cubit and a half the breadth thereof. 18 And thou shalt make two cherubims *of* gold, of beaten work shalt thou make them, in the two ends of the mercy seat. 19 And make one cherub on the one end, and the other cherub on the other end: *even* of the mercy seat shall ye make the cherubims on the two ends thereof.

20 And the cherubims shall stretch forth *their* wings on high, covering the mercy seat with their wings, and their faces *shall look* one to another; toward the mercy seat shall the faces of the cherubims be. 21 And thou shalt put the mercy seat above upon the ark; and in the ark thou shalt put the testimony that I shall give thee. 22 And there I will meet with thee, and I will commune with thee from above the mercy seat, from between the two cherubims which *are* upon the ark of the testimony, of all *things* which I will give thee in commandment unto the children of Israel.

Securing the top of the Ark was the **Mercy Seat** כַּפֹּרֶת, (*kapporeth*), a Hebrew word implying a covering. The Septuagint's ἱλαστήριον (*hilasterion*), meaning *a place* *of propitiation*, best captures the functional importance of the covering. It would be from *above the Mercy Seat* that God would meet with, and instruct, the children of Israel (vs. 22) From this seat, most likely appearing in the cloud (cf. Lev. 16:2), God would provide propitiation through the atoning blood sprinkled thereon (cf. Lev. 16:14). The Septuagint's rendering of propitiation is later applied to the sacrifice of Jesus Christ (cf. Rom. 3:25; I Jn. 2:2; 4:10). With the enthronement of God upon the Ark of the Covenant (cf. II Sam. 6:2), the connection to the New Testament believer coming *boldly before the throne of grace that we obtain mercy* (Heb. 4:16) reveals the wonderful truth of Christ becoming our way (cf. Jn. 14:6) into the place of propitiation (cf. Heb. 10:19).

The **Mercy Seat**, upon which the images of the Cherubim overshadowed the Seat, created, as it were, the *throne of God* (cf. Isa. 6:1-3; Ezek. 10) with the ark beneath referred to in scripture as God's **footstool** (I Chron. 28:2; cf. Ps. 96:5; 132:7; Isa. 66:1).

[23] Thou shalt also make a table of shittim wood: two cubits *shall be* the length thereof, and a cubit the breadth thereof, and a cubit and a half the height thereof. [24] And thou shalt overlay it with pure gold, and make thereto a crown of gold round about. [25] And thou shalt make unto it a border of an hand breadth round about, and thou shalt make a golden crown to the border thereof round about. [26] And thou shalt make for it four rings of gold, and put the rings in the four corners that *are* on the four feet thereof. [27] Over against the border shall the rings be for places of the staves to bear the table. [28] And thou shalt make the staves *of* shittim wood, and overlay them with gold, that the table may be borne with them. [29] And thou shalt make the dishes thereof, and spoons thereof,

and covers thereof, and bowls thereof, to cover withal: of pure gold shalt thou make them. ³⁰ And thou shalt set upon the table shewbread before me alway.

Thou shalt make a table of shittim wood: it would be upon the table that the **shewbread** (lit. *bread of face*) would be placed perpetually before the presence of the Lord, without the veil (Lev. 24:5-8). The table, similar to the Ark of the Covenant, was to be carried by the use of staves overlaid with gold, though they were not to permanently remain as were the staves of the Ark. The shewbread was the only actual item of food brought into the Tabernacle, since all other food and drink were offered upon the altar as cereal offerings or libations and it was to remain upon the table even during travel, though covered with badger skin, as well as, blue and scarlet cloths (Num. 4:7-8). The twelve loaves of showbread, most likely corresponding to the twelve tribes of Israel, were set out in two equal rows and replaced every week (I Chron. 9:32), while the old was to become nourishment for the priesthood (Lev. 24:5-9; cf. I Sam. 21:5-6).

³¹ And thou shalt make a candlestick *of* **pure gold:** *of* **beaten work shall the candlestick be made: his shaft, and his branches, his bowls, his knops, and his flowers, shall be of the same. ³² And six branches shall come out of the sides of it; three branches of the candlestick out of the one side, and three branches of the candlestick out of the other side: ³³ Three bowls made like unto almonds,** *with* **a knop and a flower in one branch; and three bowls made like almonds in the other branch,** *with* **a knop and a flower: so in the six branches that come out of the candlestick. ³⁴ And in the candlestick** *shall be* **four bowls made like unto almonds, with their knops and their**

flowers. ³⁵ And there *shall be a* knop under two branches of the same, and a knop under two branches of the same, and a knop under two branches of the same, according to the six branches that proceed out of the candlestick. ³⁶ Their knops and their branches shall be of the same: all it *shall be* one beaten work of pure gold. ³⁷ And thou shalt make the seven lamps thereof: and they shall light the lamps thereof, that they may give light over against it. ³⁸ And the tongs thereof, and the snuffdishes thereof, *shall be of* pure gold. ³⁹ Of a talent of pure gold shall he make it, with all these vessels. ⁴⁰ And look that thou make *them* after their pattern, which was shewed thee in the mount.

Thou shalt make a candlestick: *candlestick* is an unfortunate translation since the object was an *oil-fed lampstand* (commonly seen as a Menorah). While there is a great degree of detail vested in the design of the lampstand, its dimensions are curiously absent. Also, unlike the gold-overlaid shittim wood of the other articles of furniture, the lampstand was to be completely made of one material; **pure gold**. Its purpose, though rich with typology, was to **give light over against it**; that is to say, light to the interior of the Holy Place thus enabling the priesthood to perform the required duties within. Further inspection reveals a unique similarity in the details of the lampstand to that of a fruit-bearing tree (shaft, branches, flowers, almond-like bowls). Careful instructions would be given the priesthood for the maintenance and perpetuation of the lampstands function (Ex. 27:20; 30:7; cf. II Chron. 13:11).

Notes

Chapter 26

¹ Moreover thou shalt make the tabernacle *with* ten curtains *of* fine twined linen, and blue, and purple, and scarlet: *with* cherubims of cunning work shalt thou make them. ² The length of one curtain *shall be* eight and twenty cubits, and the breadth of one curtain four cubits: and every one of the curtains shall have one measure. ³ The five curtains shall be coupled together one to another; and *other* five curtains *shall be* coupled one to another. ⁴ And thou shalt make loops of blue upon the edge of the one curtain from the selvedge in the coupling; and likewise shalt thou make in the uttermost edge of *another* curtain, in the coupling of the second. ⁵ Fifty loops shalt thou make in the one curtain, and fifty loops shalt thou make in the edge of the curtain that *is* in the coupling of the second; that the loops may take hold one of another. ⁶ And thou shalt make fifty taches of gold, and couple the curtains together with the taches: and it shall be one tabernacle.

Thou shalt make the tabernacle: here, scripture introduces us to the elaborate *four-fold covering* of curtains that would sit upon the framework of the interconnected boards and pillars set into sockets. The **first covering**, viewed only from the inside, consisted of ten curtains (two sides of five each) that were attached by fifty loops and clasps. The finely-twined linen of blue, purple, and scarlet was woven in such a way that the visible **cunning work** (lit. *work of thought*) of cherubim would be viewed in the completed work. This covering, along with the framework, comprised the **Tabernacle** נִשְׁכָּן (*miškān*) proper.

⁷ **And thou shalt make curtains of goats'** *hair* **to be a covering upon the tabernacle: eleven curtains shalt thou make.** ⁸ **The length of one curtain** *shall be* **thirty cubits, and the breadth of one curtain four cubits: and the eleven curtains** *shall be all* **of one measure.** ⁹ **And thou shalt couple five curtains by themselves, and six curtains by themselves, and shalt double the sixth curtain in the forefront of the tabernacle.** ¹⁰ **And thou shalt make fifty loops on the edge of the one curtain** *that is* **outmost in the coupling, and fifty loops in the edge of the curtain which coupleth the second.** ¹¹ **And thou shalt make fifty taches of brass, and put the taches into the loops, and couple the tent together, that it may be one.** ¹² **And the remnant that remaineth of the curtains of the tent, the half curtain that remaineth, shall hang over the backside of the tabernacle.** ¹³ **And a cubit on the one side, and a cubit on the other side of that which remaineth in the length of the curtains of the tent, it shall hang over the sides of the tabernacle on this side and on that side, to cover it.**

Curtains of goat hair...eleven: here, the second covering of goats hair, which was of common use in Biblical times (I Sa. 19:13; 16) is mentioned. This **tent-covering,** לְאֹהֶל (*'ōhel*), served as a protective shield over the elaborate linen curtains beneath, with an extra curtain so that there would be an overlap due to the longer dimensions, thus ensuring a complete covering of the inner covering and boards, though the sockets may have remained exposed.

14 And thou shalt make a covering for the tent *of* rams' skins dyed red, and a covering above *of* badgers' skins.

A covering for the tent...and a covering above: it is *possible* that the **third covering**, הָסְכמ (*mikseh*), of **ram's skin died red** remained visible to the congregation of Israel after the erection of the Tabernacle proper and the **tent-covering,** לְהֹא (*ōhel*), of goat's hair above (cf. Ex. 40:19). However, traditional understanding places the covering of badgers' skin, most likely the water-repellent skin of seals common to the Red Sea, as the outer covering of the Tabernacle. Interestingly, scripture iterates the use of the badger's skin as **a concealing cover** for the Tabernacle, it's inner furniture, and the holy vessels and utensils during the congregation's movement through the wilderness (Num. 4).

15 And thou shalt make boards for the tabernacle *of* shittim wood standing up. 16 Ten cubits *shall be* the length of a board, and a cubit and a half *shall be* the breadth of one board. 17 Two tenons *shall there be* in one board, set in order one against another: thus shalt thou make for all the boards of the tabernacle.

Thou shalt make boards...of shittim wood standing up: the word **boards** שֶׁרֶק (*qereš*) has been widely accepted to imply **wooden frames**, rather than heavy, solid planks of shittim wood. However, they still must have been of considerable weight since they were **overlaid with gold** (Ex. 26:29; cf. 36:34). The frames were designed in such a way that they were to anchor, due to the two side-by-side tenon's (*pegs*) on the bottom end, to the silver foundational sockets.

¹⁸ And thou shalt make the boards for the tabernacle, twenty boards on the south side southward. ¹⁹ And thou shalt make forty sockets of silver under the twenty boards; two sockets under one board for his two tenons, and two sockets under another board for his two tenons. ²⁰ And for the second side of the tabernacle on the north side *there shall be* twenty boards: ²¹ And their forty sockets of silver; two sockets under one board, and two sockets under another board. ²² And for the sides of the tabernacle westward thou shalt make six boards. ²³ And two boards shalt thou make for the corners of the tabernacle in the two sides. ²⁴ And they shall be coupled together beneath, and they shall be coupled together above the head of it unto one ring: thus shall it be for them both; they shall be for the two corners. ²⁵ And they shall be eight boards, and their sockets of silver, sixteen sockets; two sockets under one board, and two sockets under another board.

Twenty boards on the Southside.... Northside: Twenty wooden frames (40 total) were located on both the northern and southern walls, and eight frames were erected along the western wall, two of which were specified as corner boards that were fastened by rings (top and bottom) to the corresponding northern and southern end boards, thus providing additional support (**vss. 22-25**).

Thou shalt make…silver sockets: The silver sockets, two for each board, numbered 96 in total. Interestingly, the source of the silver utilized in casting the sockets had been secured through the collection of the half-shekel ransom of every male over the age of twenty (Ex. 30:11-16). It could be said that the foundation of God's house was built upon the ransom of able-bodied men.

²⁶ **And thou shalt make bars** *of* **shittim wood; five for the boards of the one side of the tabernacle,** ²⁷ **And five bars for the boards of the other side of the tabernacle, and five bars for the boards of the side of the tabernacle, for the two sides westward.** ²⁸ **And the middle bar in the midst of the boards shall reach from end to end.** ²⁹ **And thou shalt overlay the boards with gold, and make their rings** *of* **gold** *for* **places for the bars: and thou shalt overlay the bars with gold.** ³⁰ **And thou shalt rear up the tabernacle according to the fashion thereof which was shewed thee in the mount.**

Thou shalt make bars: here, **bars**, בְּרִיחַ (*beriyah*) implies *crossbars*, such as the bolts used to secure gates and doors. There were five bars overlaid with gold that were to be placed through rings along the northern and southern walls with the middle bar crossing the entire length of each wall.

³¹ **And thou shalt make a vail** *of* **blue, and purple, and scarlet, and fine twined linen of cunning work: with cherubims shall it be made** ³² **And thou shalt hang it upon four pillars of shittim** *wood* **overlaid with gold: their hooks** *shall be of* **gold, upon the four sockets of silver.** ³³ **And thou shalt hang up the vail under the taches, that thou mayest bring in thither within the vail the ark of the testimony: and the vail shall divide unto you between the holy** *place* **and the most holy.**

Thou shalt make a vail: the **vail**, פָּרֹכֶת (*pāroket*) with cherubim embroidered into its fabric (like the lowest covering of the Tabernacle), was to be hung by **hooks of gold** upon **four pillars** (lit. poles) **of shittim wood overlaid with gold** set into a socket of silver, also called the *Sockets of the Sanctuary* (Ex. 38:27). This vail would come to reflect the physical partition that had come to separate man from God, similar to the cherubim that had stood at the entrance to the Garden of Eden after the expulsion of Adam and Eve (Gen. 3:24). Even after the breakdown of the Tabernacle, the Ark of the Covenant and the Mercy Seat were still to remain behind the veil, since the vail was to be wrapped around the Ark when traveling and a covering of blue placed around the veil itself (cf. Num. 4:5).

Access into the Holy of Holies was only possible once a year after the high priest had enacted all the rituals required to allow for the atoning activities upon the Mercy Seat. However, with the atoning work of Jesus Christ the veil was rent (cf. Matt. 27:51; Mark 15:38; Lk. 23:45) and *by a new and living way...through the veil* (cf. Heb. 10:20) access into the presence of God was secured where man could *draw near with a true heart in full assurance* (Heb. 10:22). Apart from Jesus Christ, no one has access into God's presence (Jn. 14:6) and, as there was only one door which led into the Tabernacle, so also does Jesus stand as the Door (Jn. 10:9).

[34] And thou shalt put the mercy seat upon the ark of the testimony in the most holy *place*. [35] And thou shalt set the table without the vail, and the candlestick over against the table on the side of the tabernacle toward the south: and thou shalt put the table on the north side.

36 And thou shalt make an hanging for the door of the tent, *of* blue, and purple, and scarlet, and fine twined

linen, wrought with needlework. 37 And thou shalt make for the hanging five pillars *of* shittim *wood*, and overlay them with gold, *and* their hooks *shall be of* gold: and thou shalt cast five sockets of brass for them.

Thou shalt make an hanging for the door: while the veil separated the Holy Place from the Holy of Holies, the courtyard and the Holy Place were separated by this **hanging,** מָסָךְ (*māsāk*), of multicolored fabric, **wrought with needlework** (similar to the inner veil and lowest covering, excluding the cherubim). This hanging would differ also in that it hung from **five poles overlaid with gold** which were set into five corresponding **brass sockets.**

Notes

Chapter 27

¹ And thou shalt make an altar *of* shittim wood, five cubits long, and five cubits broad; the altar shall be foursquare: and the height thereof *shall be* three cubits. ² And thou shalt make the horns of it upon the four corners thereof: his horns shall be of the same: and thou shalt overlay it with brass. ³ And thou shalt make his pans to receive his ashes, and his shovels, and his basons, and his fleshhooks, and his firepans: all the vessels thereof thou shalt make *of* brass. ⁴ And thou shalt make for it a grate of network *of* brass; and upon the net shalt thou make four brasen rings in the four corners thereof. ⁵ And thou shalt put it under the compass of the altar beneath, that the net may be even to the midst of the altar. ⁶ And thou shalt make staves for the altar, staves *of* shittim wood, and overlay them with brass. ⁷ And the staves shall be put into the rings, and the staves shall be upon the two sides of the altar, to bear it. ⁸ Hollow with boards shalt thou make it: as it was shewed thee in the mount, so shall they make *it*.

Thou shalt make an altar of shittim wood: here, scripture transitions to the furniture found in the court of the tabernacle. Unlike the items of the Tabernacle proper that were either pure gold or overlaid with gold, the objects of the courtyard were overlaid with bronze, (most likely copper). Commonly referred to as the *brazen altar*, it was a perfect square, hollow in the middle, featuring four **horns** in each corner that would serve to bind the sacrifice upon the altar (Ps. 118:27). Mobility of the altar was facilitated by use of **staves** placed through rings on two opposing sides of the altar. The altar featured a bronze grilling surface and an intricate meshwork of brass that hung suspended in the middle of the altar, presumably to hold the burning wood and allowing for the ashes to fall to the earth below.

⁹ And thou shalt make the court of the tabernacle: for the south side southward *there shall be* **hangings for the court** *of* **fine twined linen of an hundred cubits long for one side: ¹⁰ And the twenty pillars thereof and their twenty sockets** *shall be of* **brass; the hooks of the pillars and their fillets** *shall be of* **silver. ¹¹ And likewise for the north side in length there** *shall be* **hangings of an hundred cubits long, and his twenty pillars and their twenty sockets of brass; the hooks of the pillars and their fillets of silver. ¹² And** *for* **the breadth of the court on the west side** *shall be* **hangings of fifty cubits: their pillars ten, and their sockets ten. ¹³ And the breadth of the court on the east side eastward** *shall be* **fifty cubits. ¹⁴ The hangings of one side** *of the gate shall be* **fifteen cubits: their pillars three, and their sockets three. ¹⁵ And on the other side** *shall be* **hangings fifteen** *cubits*: **their pillars three, and their sockets three. ¹⁶ And for the gate of the court** *shall be* **an hanging of twenty cubits,** *of* **blue, and purple, and scarlet, and fine twined linen, wrought with needlework:** *and* **their pillars** *shall be* **four, and their sockets four. ¹⁷ All the pillars round about the court** *shall be* **filleted with silver; their hooks** *shall* **be** *of* **silver,**

and their sockets *of* brass. ¹⁸ The length of the court *shall be* an hundred cubits, and the breadth fifty every where, and the height five cubits *of* fine twined linen, and their sockets of brass.

Make the court of the tabernacle: the **court,** חָצֵר (*hāsēr*) was an enclosure roughly **150 feet long, 75 feet wide, and 7.5 feet high**, allowing for a large gathering of worshippers to engage in the sacrificial rituals of the Tabernacle. There was a total of 60 **pillars** and 60 corresponding **sockets.** While we know the sockets were made of brass, there is no express mention of the material of the pillars, though consistency would lend toward shittim wood. Each pillar was **filleted with silver** at the top, implying a *connecting band or rod* that linked each pillar to the following thus providing a sense of stabilization for the entire courtyard. It would be upon these connecting bands or rods that the hooks and clasps of silver would secure the hanging curtain of the courtyard. Exodus 38:17 also reveals that each pillar was crowned with a **chapiter** (lit. *head*) **of silver**. At the eastern side, a 30-foot-wide **gate**, with a hanging curtain that consisted of the same material and makeup as the hanging for the Tabernacle entrance (**v. 36**) was upheld for four pillars set into four sockets. This gate marked the first of three progressive entries, though the gate of the courtyard was the only gate non-priests could pass through.

¹⁹ All the vessels of the tabernacle in all the service thereof, and all the pins thereof, and all the pins of the court, *shall be of* brass. ²⁰ And thou shalt command the children of Israel, that they bring thee pure oil olive beaten for the light, to cause the lamp to burn always. ²¹ In the tabernacle of the congregation without the vail,

which is before the testimony, Aaron and his sons shall order it from evening to morning before the LORD: *it shall be* a statute for ever unto their generations on the behalf of the children of Israel.

Pure olive oil beaten for the light, to cause the lamp to burn always: the olive oil that was isolated for the purpose of fueling the lampstand in the Holy Place was to be the purest grade of olive oil possible, called Beaten Oil. Beaten Oil was obtained by lightly pressing very ripe olives, being careful not to crush them, and the resulting few drops were gathered and stored. After several subsequent pressings, eventually leading to the crushing of the olive to extract oil from the pulpy fruit, several grades of oil were produced. Essentially, beaten oil (first oil) was the first fruit of the olive that was *allowed to flow out of itself* before the rigors of pressing and crushing the pulp was applied.

Notes

Chapter 28

¹ **And take thou unto thee Aaron thy brother, and his sons with him, from among the children of Israel, that he may minister unto me in the priest's office,** *even* **Aaron, Nadab and Abihu, Eleazar and Ithamar, Aaron's sons.** ² **And thou shalt make holy garments for Aaron thy brother for glory and for beauty.** ³ **And thou shalt speak unto all** *that are* **wise hearted, whom I have filled with the spirit of wisdom, that they may make Aaron's garments to consecrate him, that he may minister unto me in the priest's office.** ⁴ **And these** *are* **the garments which they shall make; a breastplate, and an ephod, and a robe, and a broidered coat, a mitre, and a girdle: and they shall make holy garments for Aaron thy brother, and his sons, that he may minister unto me in the priest's office.**

Take unto thee Aaron...his sons...from among the children of Israel: here, Moses would separate Aaron and his sons from the children of Israel to install them as the mediating priesthood (cf. Lev. 8). With this separation came the instructions for garments suitable to their office, namely, **holy garments for glory and beauty** that would clearly distinguish their position among the people. Clothing often functioned to identify one's position, calling, or status within society as seen in the mantle of the prophets (I Sam. 28:14), the garments of a king (II Sam. 6:14-16, 20), and the garment of a favored son (Gen. 37:3). As to the weaving and design, the contingency of **wise-hearted** individuals **filled with the spirit of wisdom** that had been given to Bezaleel (Ex. 28:3; 35.24; 36:1) were to fashion the six garments along with the medallion (**vv. 36-38**) and undergarments (**vv. 42-43**) mentioned later.

5 And they shall take gold, and blue, and purple, and scarlet, and fine linen. 6 And they shall make the ephod *of* **gold,** *of* **blue, and** *of* **purple,** *of* **scarlet, and fine twined linen, with cunning work. 7 It shall have the two shoulderpieces thereof joined at the two edges thereof; and so it shall be joined together. 8 And the curious girdle of the ephod, which is upon it, shall be of the same, according to the work thereof;** *even of* **gold,** *of* **blue, and purple, and scarlet, and fine twined linen.**

The **ephod**, whose colors were mostly consistent with the lowest covering of the Tabernacle and the innermost separating veil (cf. Ex. 26:1;31), was a garment that reached from shoulder to thigh with shoulder straps that passed over the shoulders of the priest that were then fastened via gold settings and woven chains to the breastplate. Cinching the ephod tightly around the waist was a curious girdle, signifying a skillfully-woven belt of some sorts.

9 And thou shalt take two onyx stones, and grave on them the names of the children of Israel: 10 Six of their names on one stone, and *the other* **six names of the rest on the other stone, according to their birth. 11 With the work of an engraver in stone,** *like* **the engravings of a**

signet, shalt thou engrave the two stones with the names of the children of Israel: thou shalt make them to be set in ouches of gold. ¹² And thou shalt put the two stones upon the shoulders of the ephod *for* stones of memorial unto the children of Israel: and Aaron shall bear their names before the LORD upon his two shoulders for a memorial. ¹³ And thou shalt make ouches *of* gold; ¹⁴ And two chains *of* pure gold at the ends; *of* wreathen work shalt thou make them, and fasten the wreathen chains to the ouches.

Set them in ouches of gold: the two stones bearing the combined names of the 12 tribes of Israel were to be placed in **golden ouches**, an uncertain word that probably refers to an ornate frame of gold, much like the setting of a modern gem. These two onyx stones, placed in the golden ouches, were to be set upon each shoulder strap of the high priest for a memorial, with an additional golden ouch affixed to the end of each shoulder strap. Then, **chains** of **pure gold of woven work**, were to be set into the ouches on the end of each shoulder strap and connected to the rings in the breastplate (**vv. 22-25**).

¹⁵ And thou shalt make the breastplate of judgment with cunning work; after the work of the ephod thou shalt make it; *of* gold, *of* blue, and *of* purple, and *of* scarlet, and *of* fine twined linen, shalt thou make it. ¹⁶ Foursquare it shall be *being* doubled; a span *shall be* the length thereof, and a span *shall be* the breadth thereof. ¹⁷ And thou shalt set in it settings of stones, *even* four rows of stones: *the first* row *shall be* a sardius, a topaz, and a carbuncle: *this shall be* the first row. ¹⁸ And the second row *shall be* an emerald, a sapphire, and a diamond. ¹⁹ And the third row a ligure, an agate, and an amethyst. ²⁰

And the fourth row a beryl, and an onyx, and a jasper: they shall be set in gold in their inclosings. ²¹ And the stones shall be with the names of the children of Israel, twelve, according to their names, *like* the engravings of a signet; every one with his name shall they be according to the twelve tribes.

Thou shalt make the breastplate of judgment: **the חֹשֶׁן מִשְׁפָּט** (*hoshen mishpat*), is best translated as the *pouch of judgment*, further indicated by the foursquare nature of its design and its being **doubled** (lit. *folded*), thus creating a pocket that would hold the **Urim and Thummim** (v. 30). Upon the face of the pouch a **setting of stones** (four rows of four stones each) was to be **set in gold in their inclosings.**

²² And thou shalt make upon the breastplate chains at the ends *of* wreathen work *of* pure gold. ²³ And thou shalt make upon the breastplate two rings of gold, and shalt put the two rings on the two ends of the breastplate. ²⁴ And thou shalt put the two wreathen *chains* of gold in the two rings *which are* on the ends of the breastplate. ²⁵ And *the other* two ends of the two wreathen *chains* thou shalt fasten in the two ouches, and put them on the shoulderpieces of the ephod before it. ²⁶ And thou shalt make two rings of gold, and thou shalt put them upon the two ends of the breastplate in the border thereof, which *is* in the side of the ephod inward. ²⁷ And two *other* rings of gold thou shalt make, and shalt put them on the two sides of the ephod underneath, toward the forepart thereof, *over* against the other coupling thereof, above the curious girdle of the ephod. ²⁸ And they shall bind the breastplate by the rings thereof unto the rings of the ephod with a lace of blue, that *it* may be above

the curious girdle of the ephod, and that the breastplate be not loosed from the ephod. ²⁹ And Aaron shall bear the names of the children of Israel in the breastplate of judgment upon his heart, when he goeth in unto the holy *place*, for a memorial before the LORD continually.

Aaron shall bear the names of the children of Israel: both upon the shoulders and over the heart, Aaron and every subsequent high-priest to follow, would **bear,**אִשָּׂא (*nāśā'*), a Hebrew verb signifying the act of *lifting*, the nation of Israel (collective twelve tribes) as a memorial before the Lord continually. It was sobering to consider that the redemptive responsibility of the nation would hang upon the shoulders of the High Priest every year.

³⁰ **And thou shalt put in the breastplate of judgment the Urim and the Thummim; and they shall be upon Aaron's heart, when he goeth in before the LORD: and Aaron shall bear the judgment of the children of Israel upon his heart before the LORD continually.**

Thou shalt put in the breastplate of judgment the Urim and the Thummim: the form and nature of the Urim and the Thummim have remained a mystery. Often translated from the Hebrew as "lightings and perfections", the two stones functioned as oracular objects used to ascertain divine will (cf. Num. 27:21). In another scripture, Urim (no mention of Thummim) is equated with dreams and prophets (cf. I Sam. 28:6) and in the Book of Ezra, included the discerning of the priestly bloodline when genealogies could not be found (Ez. 2:61-63). It would seem, based on internal Biblical evidence, that the Urim and the Thummim functioned *similar* to the casting of lots, where 'what man cast from the bosom, the verdict belonged to God'.

(cf. Prov. 16:33). Elsewhere, such as the choosing of the scapegoat (Lev. 16:8), the action of using material objects to divine God's intent, will, or decision is found. The emphasis of such practices highlight a great mystery in scripture but the importance is to recognize that, in each case, *the verdict belonged to God*. Though the use of Urim and Thummim is absent from later scripture, the practice of discerning Gods will through the use of lots can still be found (cf. Acts 1:26).

³¹ And thou shalt make the robe of the ephod all *of* blue. ³² And there shall be an hole in the top of it, in the midst thereof: it shall have a binding of woven work round about the hole of it, as it were the hole of an habergeon, that it be not rent.

The robe of the ephod: beneath the ephod was to be a robe of blue with a hole for the head in the top that was secured by a **binding of woven work**. To explain this concept, there is the mention of the **hole of an habergeon**, אָרְחַת (*tahrā*), a word of uncertain origin but one that most scholars agree to mean *coat of mail*. Thus, the ephod, like a coat of mail, was to be made in such a way (one piece) that discouraged or prevented tearing, further established by the heavy binding work around the neck.

³³ And *beneath* upon the hem of it thou shalt make pomegranates *of* blue, and *of* purple, and *of* scarlet, round about the hem thereof; and bells of gold between them round about: ³⁴ A golden bell and a pomegranate, a golden bell and a pomegranate, upon the hem of the robe round about. ³⁵ And it shall be upon Aaron to minister: and his sound shall be heard when he goeth in unto the

holy *place* before the LORD, and when he cometh out, that he die not.

Upon the hem…pomegranates….bells of gold: affixed to the hem of the robe were pomegranate shapes of woven material dyed blue, purple, and scarlet. Affixed beside each woven pomegranate were golden bells, thus creating a repeating pattern of pomegranate, bell, pomegranate, bell, etc. Interestingly, though the function of the woven pomegranate is unknown, the golden bells were designed that, **his sound shall be heard…that he die not.**

This function, that **his sound be heard**, has led to various conjectures by scholars. While some believe the bells functioned to communicate the well-being of the high priest during his entrance into the Holy of Holies, the ultimate purpose, **that he die**, not leads to a simpler idea. Obviously, the bells corresponded to the actions and service of the high priest in such a way that would constantly remind him of his steps and progress through the important rituals of yearly atonement. The slight tinkle of each step would surely serve to keep the high priest's attention to each detail of service, being careful to strictly adhere to divine pattern, unlike Hophni and Phinehas.

³⁶ **And thou shalt make a plate** *of* **pure gold, and grave upon it,** *like* **the engravings of a signet, HOLINESS TO THE LORD.** ³⁷ **And thou shalt put it on a blue lace, that it may be upon the mitre; upon the forefront of the mitre it shall be.** ³⁸ **And it shall be upon Aaron's forehead, that Aaron may bear the iniquity of the holy things, which the children of Israel shall hallow in all their holy gifts;**

and it shall be always upon his forehead, that they may be accepted before the LORD.

The **plate**, אְרָחַת (taḥrā'), a Hebrew word meaning *flower or blossom*, is best understood as a shining gold plate that extended across the forehead, ear to ear. Engraved into the golden plate were to be the words, קֹדֶשׁ לַיהוָה, *Holy to YHWH*, like a signet, indicating the manner of being permanently and meticulously etched into the gold. The engraved golden plate would then be affixed to a **blue lace** (lit. *cord*) which, in turn, would go around the **mitre** (lit. *turban*) of the high priest.

[39] And thou shalt embroider the coat of fine linen, and thou shalt make the mitre *of* fine linen, and thou shalt make the girdle *of* needlework. [40] And for Aaron's sons thou shalt make coats, and thou shalt make for them girdles, and bonnets shalt thou make for them, for glory and for beauty.

Embroider the coat: here the well-known **tunic** כֻּתֹּנֶת, (*kuttōnet*) is mentioned. The *kuttōnet* was a garment worn by both men and women, often as an ankle-length garment (II Sam. 15:32; Song 5:3), whose first mention is of the fur-made tunics of Adam and Eve (Gen. 3:21). In many cases the tunic was of a linen-like material and was worn as a layer of clothing beneath an outer garment, often the garment torn in moments of grief and mourning (II Sam. 15:32). The girdle was a belt-like sash and the **bonnet**, a different Hebrew word than that of the mitre of the High Priest, was believed to be flattened type of cap utilized by the ordinary priesthood that only partially covered the head.

[41] And thou shalt put them upon Aaron thy brother, and his sons with him; and shalt anoint them, and consecrate

them, and sanctify them, that they may minister unto me in the priest's office.

⁴² And thou shalt make them linen breeches to cover their nakedness; from the loins even unto the thighs they shall reach: ⁴³ And they shall be upon Aaron, and upon his sons, when they come in unto the tabernacle of the congregation, or when they come near unto the altar to minister in the holy *place*; that they bear not iniquity, and die: *it shall be* a statute for ever unto him and his seed after him.

Thou shalt make them linen breeches to cover their nakedness: the **breeches,** מִכְנָסַיִם (*miknāsayim*), are only mentioned in scripture as they relate to the priestly attire, though similar garments were known to be used historically by others than the priestly office. The express purpose of the linen undergarments was to avoid the priesthood from exposing their nakedness, from **loins even unto the thighs**, while walking up the steps or ramp of the altar while administering the rituals of the Tabernacle.

Notes

Chapter 29

¹ And this *is* the thing that thou shalt do unto them to hallow them, to minister unto me in the priest's office: Take one young bullock, and two rams without blemish, ² And unleavened bread, and cakes unleavened tempered with oil, and wafers unleavened anointed with oil: *of* wheaten flour shalt thou make them. ³ And thou shalt put them into one basket, and bring them in the basket, with the bullock and the two rams. ⁴ And Aaron and his sons thou shalt bring unto the door of the tabernacle of the congregation, and shalt wash them with water. ⁵ And thou shalt take the garments, and put upon Aaron the coat, and the robe of the ephod, and the ephod, and the breastplate, and gird him with the curious girdle of the ephod: ⁶ And thou shalt put the mitre upon his head, and put the holy crown upon the mitre. ⁷ Then shalt thou take the anointing oil, and pour it upon his head, and anoint him. ⁸ And thou shalt bring his sons, and put coats upon them. ⁹ And thou shalt gird them with girdles, Aaron and his sons, and put the bonnets on them: and the priest's office shall be theirs for a perpetual statute: and thou shalt consecrate Aaron and his sons. ¹⁰ And thou shalt cause a bullock to be brought before the tabernacle of the congregation: and Aaron and his sons shall put their hands upon the head of the bullock.

Put their hands upon the head of the bullock: the ritual of **laying** סָמַךְ (*sāmak*) one's hand upon the head of the sacrifice is more accurately translated as *"to lean upon."* This gesture typically served as a means of vicarious substitution between the offeror and the offering (Lev. 16:21; Num. 8:12). However, this activity (the laying on of hands) was not isolated to animal-specific offerings serving as vicarious substitutions. Instead, the activity is found in association with the appointment of successors where the appointer lays his hands upon the appointee, as seen in the transfer of power between Moses and Joshua (cf. Deut. 34:9). Even then, the emphasis of *transfer* remains the underlying function of the action. This symbolic action of hand laying is also found in the New Testament where the aspect of *transfer* remains the underlying premise of the gesture (Acts 8:18; I Tim. 4:14; II Tim. 1:6).

[11] **And thou shalt kill the bullock before the LORD,** *by* **the door of the tabernacle of the congregation.** [12] **And thou shalt take of the blood of the bullock, and put it upon the horns of the altar with thy finger, and pour all the blood beside the bottom of the altar.** [13] **And thou shalt take all the fat that covereth the inwards, and the caul** *that is* **above the liver, and the two kidneys, and the fat that** *is* **upon them, and burn** *them* **upon the altar.** [14] **But the flesh of the bullock, and his skin, and his dung, shalt thou burn with fire without the camp: it** *is* **a sin offering.** [15] **Thou shalt also take one ram; and Aaron and his sons shall put their hands upon the head of the ram.** [16] **And thou shalt slay the ram, and thou shalt take his blood, and sprinkle** *it* **round about upon the altar.** [17] **And thou shalt cut the ram in pieces, and wash the inwards of him, and his legs, and put** *them* **unto his pieces, and unto his head.** [18] **And thou shalt burn the whole ram upon the**

altar: it *is* a burnt offering unto the LORD: it is a sweet savour, an offering made by fire unto the LORD. [19] And thou shalt take the other ram; and Aaron and his sons shall put their hands upon the head of the ram. [20] Then shalt thou kill the ram, and take of his blood, and put *it* upon the tip of the right ear of Aaron, and upon the tip of the right ear of his sons, and upon the thumb of their right hand, and upon the great toe of their right foot, and sprinkle the blood upon the altar round about. [21] And thou shalt take of the blood that *is* upon the altar, and of the anointing oil, and sprinkle *it* upon Aaron, and upon his garments, and upon his sons, and upon the garments of his sons with him: and he shall be hallowed, and his garments, and his sons, and his sons' garments with him.

Thou shalt take the other ram...: Following the **sin offering** involving the bullock (vv. 11-14) and the dedicatory **burnt offering** involving a ram (vv. 15-18), a second ram was slain and a threefold application of the blood of this ram was applied to the **right ear, right thumb, and right great toe**. The key to understanding these actions is found in that the ram is called the **ram of consecration** (v. 22), literally a *ram of ordination*. This threefold application of blood taken from the ram of ordination served to dedicate the whole priest to the service of the house of God (cf. Lev. 14:14). The feature of blood throughout the process of priestly installment dominates the ceremony. It is wiped upon the horns of the altar, poured at the base of the altar, sprinkled upon the sides of the altar, applied threefold to the specified right-oriented body parts of the priests, and sprinkled (mixed with oil) upon the priests.

[22] Also thou shalt take of the ram the fat and the rump, and the fat that covereth the inwards, and the caul *above* the

liver, and the two kidneys, and the fat that *is* upon them, and the right shoulder; for it *is* a ram of consecration: ²³ And one loaf of bread, and one cake of oiled bread, and one wafer out of the basket of the unleavened bread that *is* before the LORD: ²⁴ And thou shalt put all in the hands of Aaron, and in the hands of his sons; and shalt wave them *for* a wave offering before the LORD. ²⁵ And thou shalt receive them of their hands, and burn *them* upon the altar for a burnt offering, for a sweet savour before the LORD: it *is* an offering made by fire unto the LORD. ²⁶ And thou shalt take the breast of the ram of Aaron's consecration, and wave it *for* a wave offering before the LORD: and it shall be thy part. ²⁷ And thou shalt sanctify the breast of the wave offering, and the shoulder of the heave offering, which is waved, and which is heaved up, of the ram of the consecration, *even* of *that* which *is* for Aaron, and of *that* which is for his sons: ²⁸ And it shall be Aaron's and his sons' by a statute for ever from the children of Israel: for it *is* an heave offering: and it shall be an heave offering from the children of Israel of the sacrifice of their peace offerings, *even* their heave offering unto the LORD. ²⁹ And the holy garments of Aaron shall be his sons' after him, to be anointed therein, and to be consecrated in them. ³⁰ *And* that son that is priest in his stead shall put them on seven days, when he cometh into the tabernacle of the congregation to minister in the holy *place*. ³¹ And thou shalt take the ram of the consecration, and seethe his flesh in the holy place. ³² And Aaron and his sons shall eat the flesh of the ram, and the bread that *is* in the basket, *by* the door of the tabernacle of the congregation. ³³ And they shall eat those things wherewith the atonement was made, to consecrate *and* to sanctify them: but a stranger shall not eat *thereof*, because they *are* holy. ³⁴ And if ought of the flesh of the consecrations, or of the bread, remain unto the morning, then thou shalt burn the remainder with fire: it shall not be eaten, because it *is* holy.

Aaron and his sons shall eat the flesh of the ram: the process of consecration and sanctification, having already gone through the tedious process of the diverse applications of blood, would involve, at its essential level, a ceremonial meal of ratification (cf. Ex. 24:6-11). However, a deeper consideration is that the process of ordination would have marked the priest, *inwardly and outwardly*, by the process he undertook to be installed. The flesh the priest consumed was holy and its leftovers were to be burned so that none but the priesthood could consume them.

³⁵ And thus shalt thou do unto Aaron, and to his sons, according to all *things* which I have commanded thee: seven days shalt thou consecrate them. ³⁶ And thou shalt offer every day a bullock *for* a sin offering for atonement: and thou shalt cleanse the altar, when thou hast made an atonement for it, and thou shalt anoint it, to sanctify it. ³⁷ Seven days thou shalt make an atonement for the altar, and sanctify it; and it shall be an altar most holy: whatsoever toucheth the altar shall be holy. ³⁸ Now this *is that* which thou shalt offer upon the altar; two lambs of the first year day by day continually. ³⁹ The one lamb thou shalt offer in the morning; and the other lamb thou shalt offer at even: ⁴⁰ And with the one lamb a tenth deal of flour mingled with the fourth part of an hin of beaten oil; and the fourth part of an hin of wine *for* a drink offering. ⁴¹ And the other lamb thou shalt offer at even, and shalt do thereto according to the meat offering of the morning, and according to the drink offering thereof, for a sweet savour, an offering made by fire unto the LORD. ⁴² *This shall be* a continual burnt offering throughout

your generations *at* the door of the tabernacle of the congregation before the LORD: where I will meet you, to speak there unto thee. [43] And there I will meet with the children of Israel, and *the tabernacle* shall be sanctified by my glory. [44] And I will sanctify the tabernacle of the congregation, and the altar: I will sanctify also both Aaron and his sons, to minister to me in the priest's office. [45] And I will dwell among the children of Israel, and will be their God. [46] And they shall know that I *am* the LORD their God, that brought them forth out of the land of Egypt, that I may dwell among them: I *am* the LORD their God.

Notes

Chapter 30

¹ And thou shalt make an altar to burn incense upon: of shittim wood shalt thou make it. ² A cubit *shall be* the length thereof, and a cubit the breadth thereof; foursquare shall it be: and two cubits *shall be* the height thereof: the horns thereof *shall be* of the same. ³ And thou shalt overlay it with pure gold, the top thereof, and the sides thereof round about, and the horns thereof; and thou shalt make unto it a crown of gold round about. ⁴ And two golden rings shalt thou make to it under the crown of it, by the two corners thereof, upon the two sides of it shalt thou make *it*; and they shall be for places for the staves to bear it withal. ⁵ And thou shalt make the staves *of* shittim wood, and overlay them with gold. ⁶ And thou shalt put it before the vail that *is* by the ark of the testimony, before the mercy seat that *is* over the testimony, where I will meet with thee. ⁷ And Aaron shall burn thereon sweet incense every morning: when he dresseth the lamps, he shall burn incense upon it. ⁸ And when Aaron lighteth the lamps at even, he shall burn incense upon it, a perpetual incense before the LORD throughout your generations. ⁹ Ye shall offer no strange incense thereon, nor burnt sacrifice, nor meat offering; neither shall ye pour drink offering thereon. ¹⁰ And Aaron shall make an atonement upon the horns

of it once in a year with the blood of the sin offering of atonements: once in the year shall he make atonement upon it throughout your generations: it *is* most holy unto the LORD.

And thou shalt make an altar to burn incense: though called an **altar,** מִזְבֵּחַ (*mizbēah*), a word that signifies *a place of slaughter*, this altar was unconventional in that its only function was the exclusive burning of a specific incense made according to a specific formula (cf. Ex. 30:34-36). Since the incense was to burn perpetually, a strict schedule was implemented for its care. Every morning and evening, Aaron was to **dress** (lit. *make good*) the golden candelabra followed by burning incense upon the golden altar. Perhaps the timing of this event was to ensure that the offensive smells that resulted from the trimming and wicking of the candelabra were extinguished and replaced with sweet, lavish scent from a freshly burning incense before the Lord.

The cloud of smoke produced by the incense was to cover the mercy seat within the Holy of Holies (cf. Lev 16:13) to ensure that the High Priest remain alive. Figuratively, incense is seen throughout scripture as ascending prayer (cf. Psalm 141:2; Lk. 1:10) and specifically identified with the prayers of the saints (cf. Rev. 5:8; 8:3). Once a year, on the Day of Atonement, the blood of the sacrifice was to be sprinkled upon the horns of the Golden Altar, indeed producing a living, perpetual sweet savor unto the Lord.

[11] And the LORD spake unto Moses, saying, [12] When thou takest the sum of the children of Israel after their number, then shall they give every man a ransom for his

soul unto the LORD, when *thou* numberest them; that there be no plague among them, when thou numberest them. ¹³ This they shall give, every one that passeth among them that are numbered, half a shekel after the shekel of the sanctuary: (a shekel *is* twenty gerahs:) an half shekel *shall be* the offering of the LORD. ¹⁴ Every one that passeth among them that are numbered, from twenty years old and above, shall give an offering unto the LORD. ¹⁵ The rich shall not give more, and the poor shall not give less than half a shekel, when *they* give an offering unto the LORD, to make an atonement for your souls. ¹⁶ And thou shalt take the atonement money of the children of Israel, and shalt appoint it for the service of the tabernacle of the congregation; that it may be a memorial unto the children of Israel before the LORD, to make an atonement for your souls.

When thou takest the sum of the children of Israel: it is here that the numbering of males, twenty years and up, is referred as a census (cf. Num. 1:3). Such census demanded the strict adherence of a half-shekel ransom for each male that was counted so **that there be no plague among you**. The key to understanding this is found in **v. 14; everyone that passeth among them** (lit. *crosses over*). The act of a census was a literal *crossing over* that necessitated every man forsake his own life for God, thus demanding a ransom that would purchase back his life. The failure to call for a census without instituting a ransom would be found in later scripture, thus opening the door for wide-spread plague (II Sam. 24).

¹⁷ And the LORD spake unto Moses, saying, 18 Thou shalt also make a laver *of* brass, and his foot *also of* brass, to wash *withal*: and thou shalt put it between the tabernacle of the congregation and the altar, and thou

shalt put water therein. ¹⁹ For Aaron and his sons shall wash their hands and their feet thereat: ²⁰ When they go into the tabernacle of the congregation, they shall wash with water, that they die not; or when they come near to the altar to minister, to burn offering made by fire unto the LORD: ²¹ So they shall wash their hands and their feet, that they die not: and it shall be a statute for ever to them, *even* to him and to his seed throughout their generations.

Laver of brass: Located just outside of the tent in the courtyard the laver (lit. *washstand*) served to prepare the priesthood for the holy ministrations of Tabernacle service. The laver and its base were made of the brass (some believe copper) secured from the lookingglasses (lit. *vision*, implying mirrors) of the woman that gathered at the door of the Tabernacle (cf. Ex. 25:3; 38:8). This would indicate that both the washstand and base were reflective and the priests could observe their images and actions while washing. Every holy service, beginning with the Altar of Burnt Offering, was to be preceded by the preparation of washing, **that they die not** (vss. 20-21). This activity of washing was declared to be a **statute forever** to Aaron and his descendants and one whose symbolism is to be demonstrated daily in the life of the New Testament believer (Jn. 13:10).

²² Moreover the LORD spake unto Moses, saying, ²³ Take thou also unto thee principal spices, of pure myrrh five hundred *shekels*, and of sweet cinnamon half so much, *even* two hundred and fifty *shekels*, and of sweet calamus two hundred and fifty *shekels*, ²⁴ And of cassia five hundred *shekels*, after the shekel of the sanctuary, and of oil olive an hin: ²⁵ And thou shalt make it an oil

of holy ointment, an ointment compound after the art of the apothecary: it shall be an holy anointing oil.

Take unto thee principle spices: here, four choice spices mixed with oil were utilized in the creation of the **holy anointing oil** that was to be an **ointment compound after the art** (lit. *work*) **of the apothecary**. Specific commandment designated that the exclusive ingredients of the anointing oil not be utilized upon any persons other than the priesthood nor was there to be any attempt to compound **after its composition;** (vv. 31-33) the penalty there being cut off from the people of Israel.

²⁶ And thou shalt anoint the tabernacle of the congregation therewith, and the ark of the testimony, ²⁷ And the table and all his vessels, and the candlestick and his vessels, and the altar of incense, ²⁸ And the altar of burnt offering with all his vessels, and the laver and his foot. ²⁹ And thou shalt sanctify them, that they may be most holy: whatsoever toucheth them shall be holy. ³⁰ And thou shalt anoint Aaron and his sons, and consecrate them, that *they* may minister unto me in the priest's office. ³¹ And thou shalt speak unto the children of Israel, saying, This shall be an holy anointing oil unto me throughout your generations. ³² Upon man's flesh shall it not be poured, neither shall ye make *any other* like it, after the composition of it: it is holy, *and* it shall be holy unto you. ³³ Whosoever compoundeth *any* like it, or whosoever putteth *any* of it upon a stranger, shall even be cut off from his people.

³⁴ And the LORD said unto Moses, Take unto thee sweet spices, stacte, and onycha, and galbanum; *these* sweet spices with pure frankincense: of each shall there

be a like *weight*: ³⁵ And thou shalt make it a perfume, a confection after the art of the apothecary, tempered together, pure and holy: ³⁶ And thou shalt beat *some* of it very small, and put of it before the testimony in the tabernacle of the congregation, where I will meet with thee: it shall be unto you most holy. ³⁷ And *as for* the perfume which thou shalt make, ye shall not make to yourselves according to the composition thereof: it shall be unto thee holy for the LORD. ³⁸ Whosoever shall make like unto that, to smell thereto, shall even be cut off from his people.

Take unto thee sweet spices...: here, in contrast to the principles spices of the holy anointing oil, **sweet spices** (lit. aromatic spices) were to be utilized in the development of the incense. The instructions called for the spices to be **tempered together** מְמֻלָּח, (*mĕmullāh*), lit. *salted*, implying the addition of salt to the mixture thus extending the burning time and quality of the incense mixture. Instructions were also given to **beat** (lit. *pulverize*) some of the mixture to be placed upon the golden altar for the incense offering. Just as the anointing oil was not allowed to be duplicated, so also was the mixture of incense. If one were to make anything similar that bore the same smell of the mixture, they would be cut off from the camp of God.

Notes

Chapter 31

¹ And the LORD spake unto Moses, saying, ² See, I have called by name Bezaleel the son of Uri, the son of Hur, of the tribe of Judah: ³ And I have filled him with the spirit of God, in wisdom, and in understanding, and in knowledge, and in all manner of workmanship, ⁴ To devise cunning works, to work in gold, and in silver, and in brass, ⁵ And in cutting of stones, to set *them*, and in carving of timber, to work in all manner of workmanship. ⁶ And I, behold, I have given with him Aholiab, the son of Ahisamach, of the tribe of Dan: and in the hearts of all that are wise hearted I have put wisdom, that they may make all that I have commanded thee; ⁷ The tabernacle of the congregation, and the ark of the testimony, and the mercy seat that *is* thereupon, and all the furniture of the tabernacle, ⁸ And the table and his furniture, and the pure candlestick with all his furniture, and the altar of incense, ⁹ And the altar of burnt offering with all his furniture, and the laver and his foot, ¹⁰ And the cloths of service, and the holy garments for Aaron the priest, and the garments of his sons, to minister in the priest's office, ¹¹ And the anointing oil, and sweet incense for the holy *place*: according to all that I have commanded thee shall they do.

I have called by name Bezaleel: even though the Levites would carry the charge of Tabernacle service, God would appoint a **Judahite** as the foreman of the Tabernacle's construction. While the Levites were commissioned through lineage, Bezaleel was chosen due to his being **filled with the spirit of God** and, due to this, having **wisdom, understanding,** and **knowledge** in **all manner of workmanship** associated with the construction of the Tabernacle. The idiomatic phrase, **filled with the spirit of God** as it related to the dispensation of Bezaleel, should not be confused with the New Testament phenomenon of regenerative spirit-infilling (Acts 2:1-4).

Instead, the qualities of wisdom, understanding, and knowledge were the result of Bezaleels being empowered by the Spirit of God to accomplish the divine task of constructing the Tabernacle, its furniture, and all other instruments according to the blueprint God had given Moses (cf. Jdg. 14:6; I Sam. 16:13). It is probable that Bezaleel was already a gifted craftsman, though the divine qualities would have moved him into a dimension of genius (as was found of King Solomon). This is further established in the endowment of divine wisdom placed upon Bezaleel's assistant, **Aholiab the Danite**, and those naturally **wise hearted** (v. 6).

¹² And the LORD spake unto Moses, saying, ¹³ Speak thou also unto the children of Israel, saying, Verily my sabbaths ye shall keep: for it *is* a sign between me and you throughout your generations; that *ye* may know that I *am* the LORD that doth sanctify you. ¹⁴ Ye shall keep the sabbath therefore; for it *is* holy unto you: every one that defileth it shall surely be put to death: for whosoever doeth *any* work therein, that soul shall be cut off from

among his people. ¹⁵ Six days may work be done; but in the seventh is the sabbath of rest, holy to the LORD: whosoever doeth *any* work in the sabbath day, he shall surely be put to death.

He shall surely be put to death: reflecting the verbiage given to Adam in relation to the forbidden tree (cf. Gen. 2:17), God expressed the same penalty upon those who worked on the Sabbath. It is important to note that this penalty was reserved for those who *willfully, and presumptuously* violated the commandment of God to work on the Sabbath (cf. Num. 15:28-36). A further, though often overlooked concept is also found here. Even though God desired the construction of the Tabernacle, even God's house and the work associated with His house would submit to the requirement of the Sabbath rest.

¹⁶Wherefore the children of Israel shall keep the sabbath, to observe the sabbath throughout their generations, *for* a perpetual covenant. ¹⁷ It *is* a sign between me and the children of Israel for ever: for *in* six days the LORD made heaven and earth, and on the seventh day he rested, and was refreshed. ¹⁸ And he gave unto Moses, when he had made an end of communing with him upon mount Sinai, two tables of testimony, tables of stone, written with the finger of God.

It is a sign between me and the children of Israel: here there is a reiteration of the commandment of 20:8-11(*see also the commentary for further explanation between creation, the Sabbath, and the sign*).

Notes

CHAPTER 32

¹ And when the people saw that Moses delayed to come down out of the mount, the people gathered themselves together unto Aaron, and said unto him, Up, make us gods, which shall go before us; for *as for* this Moses, the man that brought us up out of the land of Egypt, we wot not what is become of him.

The people gathered themselves together: a break in the narrative of Exodus juxtaposes itself against the backdrop of God's establishment of covenantal law and desired dwelling. Seeing that Moses delayed, the people **gathered themselves together** and demanded of Aaron, **Up, make us gods**: It should be noted, that the people are never revealed to be demanding the specific fashioning of a golden calf, but rather, they demanded that Aaron make (lit. *create*) them god(s) that would take the place of Moses, the intermediary of YHWH. Their expression of impatience reveals, to some degree, their true ignorance of Moses' position within the redemptive plan of God, and further, the lingering effects of Egypt's false religious system. Prior to this instance, the mindset of the people is revealed in that they believed deity could only be communicated with through the office of an intermediary (cf. Ex. 20:19).

² And Aaron said unto them, Break off the golden earrings, which *are* in the ears of your wives, of your sons, and of your daughters, and bring *them* unto me. ³ And all the people brake off the golden earrings which *were* in their ears, and brought *them* unto Aaron.

Break off the golden earrings: the golden earrings, secured from the Egyptians when Israel left Egypt (**11:2-3; 12:35-36**), are items loosely associated in scripture with pagan idolatry (cf. Gen. 35:4). In later scripture, Gideon would fashion a golden ephod from golden earrings, thus creating what would become a *snare* to his household and lineage (Jdg. 8:24-27).

⁴ And he received *them* at their hand, and fashioned it with a graving tool, after he had made it a molten calf: and they said, These *be* thy gods, O Israel, which brought thee up out of the land of Egypt.

Aaron...made it a molten calf: in clear violation of the Decalogue (Ex. 20:3-5), Aaron fashioned the gold he had secured from the wives and children of *the men set on mischief* (**v. 22**) into the likeness of a calf. According to Psalms 106:19-20 they, *changed glory into the likeness of an ox that eateth grass...ignoring their savior.* Consequently, God would bring an arrogant king down to the level of an ox that ate grass in late scripture (Dan. 4:33). Another event involving the fashioning of golden calves is recorded during the divided kingdom of Israel, with King Jeroboam seeking to replace the authorized worship that was centralized in Jerusalem (cf. I Kings 12).

These be thy gods, O Israel: this proclamation has long puzzled commentators since the calf never appeared to be a replacement for God, but rather, a substitute for the intermediary figure of Moses (**v. 1**). Perhaps the most substantial understanding of this event can be couched in their former demand for distance from the presence and voice of God (**vv. 20:15-16**). In other words, drawing together the pieces of this scenario and their fear at the absence of Yahweh's intermediary (Moses), they sought to fashion something that would take the place of Moses' mediatory status with God. Such logic would have fit well into the pagan ideologies of Ancient Near Eastern beliefs, where the gods were never to be approached except through an accepted medium or agency.

5 And when Aaron saw *it*, he built an altar before it; and Aaron made proclamation, and said, To morrow *is* a feast to the LORD.

He built an altar: this reaction seems out of place in the narrative of idolatrous activity, for God had made it clear that burnt offerings and sacrifices were to be only made exclusively to Him (Ex. 22:19). However, this may add further evidence of the nature of the golden calf and the still deeply pagan influence upon the people, especially in light of the presence of a mixed multitude.

⁶ And they rose up early on the morrow, and offered burnt offerings, and brought peace offerings; and the people sat down to eat and to drink, and rose up to play.

Rose up to play: following the burnt and peace offerings upon the altar that Aaron had built, the people **rose up to play**. The usage of **play**, קָחַצ (*sāhaq*), carries implications of sexual deviance, lending toward the unrestrained lasciviousness that was customary of rituals associated with many pagan cultic religions. The people had grievously intermarried Yahwistic offerings with the shining figure of a golden calf and pagan perversion, thus provoking the jealousy and anger of God.

[7] And the LORD said unto Moses, Go, get thee down; for thy people, which thou broughtest out of the land of Egypt, have corrupted *themselves*: [8] They have turned aside quickly out of the way which I commanded them: they have made them a molten calf, and have worshipped it, and have sacrificed thereunto, and said, These *be* thy gods, O Israel, which have brought thee up out of the land of Egypt. [9] And the LORD said unto Moses, I have seen this people, and, behold, it is a stiffnecked people: [10] Now therefore let me alone, that my wrath may wax hot against them, and that I may consume them: and I will make of thee a great nation.

[11] And Moses besought the LORD his God, and said, LORD, why doth thy wrath wax hot against thy people, which thou hast brought forth out of the land of Egypt with great power, and with a mighty hand? [12] Wherefore should the Egyptians speak, and say, For mischief did he bring them out, to slay them in the mountains, and to consume them from the face of the earth? Turn from thy fierce wrath, and repent of this evil against thy people. [13] Remember Abraham, Isaac, and Israel, thy servants, to whom thou swarest by thine own self, and saidst unto them, I will multiply your seed as the stars of heaven, and all this land that I have spoken of will I give unto your seed, and they shall inherit *it* for ever. [14] And the LORD repented of the evil which he thought to do unto his people.

Never once does Moses seek to justify the actions of the Israelites, but instead, he reminds God of the dramatic deliverance of the firstborn of God from Egypt. Appealing again to the promises given to Abraham, Isaac, and Jacob, the very reason for which God delivered them from Egypt to begin with, Moses interceded for the nation of Israel until God changed His mind.

15 And Moses turned, and went down from the mount, and the two tables of the testimony *were* in his hand: the tables *were* written on both their sides; on the one side and on the other were they written. 16 And the tables *were* the work of God, and the writing was the writing of God, graven upon the tables. 17 And when Joshua heard the noise of the people as they shouted, he said unto Moses, *There is* a noise of war in the camp. 18 And he said, *It is* not the voice of *them that* shout for mastery, neither *is it* the voice of *them that* cry for being overcome: *but* the noise of *them that* sing do I hear.

Moses, having already been informed of the corruption of the people, does nothing to inform Joshua of the perceived sounds that are ascending the mountain from those engaging in idolatrous worship and licentious sin. One can only imagine the thoughts that were running through the mind of Moses, perhaps not fully grasping the nature of the Israelite's sin.

19 And it came to pass, as soon as he came nigh unto the camp, that he saw the calf, and the dancing: and Moses' anger waxed hot, and he cast the tables out of his hands, and brake them beneath the mount. 20 And he took the calf which they had made, and burnt *it* in the fire, and ground *it* to powder, and strawed *it* upon the water, and made the children of Israel drink *of it*. 21 And Moses said unto Aaron, What did this people unto thee, that thou

hast brought so great a sin upon them? ²² **And Aaron said, Let not the anger of my lord wax hot: thou knowest the people, that they** *are set* **on mischief.** ²³ **For they said unto me, Make us gods, which shall go before us: for** *as for* **this Moses, the man that brought us up out of the land of Egypt, we wot not what is become of him.** ²⁴ **And I said unto them, Whosoever hath any gold, let them break** *it* **off. So they gave** *it* **me: then I cast it into the fire, and there came out this calf.**

Juxtaposed against the anger of God the anger of Moses, having now seen the severity of the people's sin, flares to life and he throws the tablets out of his hands breaking them beneath the mountain. This action revealed in literal type the very thing that the people of Israel had done; breaking the commandment of God which they had prior agreed to. Now, with shattered tablets laying at the foot of the mountain, Moses reduced the image of the calf to powder and cast the remains into the river that flowed from the side of the Mount of God making the offenders to ingest the remnants of their sin. This is reminiscent of the trial of the suspected adulteress that was to drink bitter water mingled with dust (Num. 5:12-31).

²⁵ **And when Moses saw that the people** *were* **naked; (for Aaron had made them naked unto** *their* **shame among their enemies:)**

Saw that the people were naked: here naked עָרֻפ (*para*) means to be *let loose*. In other words, Aaron had done nothing to restrain the people.

²⁶ **Then Moses stood in the gate of the camp, and said, Who** *is* **on the LORD'S side?** *let him come* **unto me. And**

all the sons of Levi gathered themselves together unto him. ²⁷ And he said unto them, Thus saith the LORD God of Israel, Put every man his sword by his side, *and* go in and out from gate to gate throughout the camp, and slay every man his brother, and every man his companion, and every man his neighbour. ²⁸ And the children of Levi did according to the word of Moses: and there fell of the people that day about three thousand men. ²⁹ For Moses had said, Consecrate yourselves to day to the LORD, even every man upon his son, and upon his brother; that he may bestow upon you a blessing this day. ³⁰ And it came to pass on the morrow, that Moses said unto the people, Ye have sinned a great sin: and now I will go up unto the LORD; peradventure I shall make an atonement for your sin. ³¹ And Moses returned unto the LORD, and said, Oh, this people have sinned a great sin, and have made them gods of gold. ³² Yet now, if thou wilt forgive their sin--; and if not, blot me, I pray thee, out of thy book which thou hast written. ³³ And the LORD said unto Moses, Whosoever hath sinned against me, him will I blot out of my book.

Judgment had been swift, 3,000 men having been slain, and the Levites stood as the only tribe that had refrained from engaging in the perverse activities of idolatrous veneration. Having gone to God to seek reconciliation for the nation of Israel, Moses reasoned with God by saying, **if thou wilt not forgive their sin... blot me...out of thy book**: more than likely Moses here speaks of the register that would become a part of the administration of the nation of Israel (called genealogies) in which the children of Israel were numbered by tribes. Further meaning and elaboration of this book is found throughout scripture, called also the Book of Life, where the record of those faithful and obedience to God and His word is found (cf. Dan. 12:1; Mal. 3:16; Phil. 4:3; Rev. 3:5; 13:8; 17:8; 20:12). Able is revealed as the first to be recorded (Heb. 11:4), and the book speaks strongly of those whom God knows belong to Him (cf. II Tim. 2:19).

³⁴ Therefore now go, lead the people unto *the place* of which I have spoken unto thee: behold, mine Angel shall go before thee: nevertheless in the day when I visit I will visit their sin upon them. ³⁵ And the LORD plagued the people, because they made the calf, which Aaron made.

Nevertheless in the day when I visit I will visit their sin upon them: though for a space of time judgment would be stayed, God full well knew the hearts of the people that had sinned and knew that a future visitation would come with future judgment to a faithfulness and disobedient generation.

Notes

CHAPTER 33

¹ And the LORD said unto Moses, Depart, *and* go up hence, thou and the people which thou hast brought up out of the land of Egypt, unto the land which I sware unto Abraham, to Isaac, and to Jacob, saying, Unto thy seed will I give it: ² And I will send an angel before thee; and I will drive out the Canaanite, the Amorite, and the Hittite, and the Perizzite, the Hivite, and the Jebusite: ³ Unto a land flowing with milk and honey: for I will not go up in the midst of thee; for thou *art* a stiffnecked people: lest I consume thee in the way. ⁴ And when the people heard these evil tidings, they mourned: and no man did put on him his ornaments. ⁵ For the LORD had said unto Moses, Say unto the children of Israel, Ye *are* a stiffnecked people: I will come up into the midst of thee in a moment, and consume thee: therefore now put off thy ornaments from thee, that I may know what to do unto thee. ⁶ And the children of Israel stripped themselves of their ornaments by the mount Horeb.

The language of v.1 is startling in that God does not refer to Israel as *my people* but **the people**. The anger of God over the actions of the Israelites leads to His removal from the congregational camp and the threat to no longer go up in their midst, but instead, merely remain an agency far ahead of them thus avoiding their **stiffnecked** ways **lest I consume thee in the way**. Israel, stripped of all ornaments of status and sonship, is grieved to hear of God's intentions and the mourn.

[7] And Moses took the tabernacle, and pitched it without the camp, afar off from the camp, and called it the Tabernacle of the congregation. And it came to pass, *that* every one which sought the LORD went out unto the tabernacle of the congregation, which *was* without the camp. [8] And it came to pass, when Moses went out unto the tabernacle, *that* all the people rose up, and stood every man at his tent door, and looked after Moses, until he was gone into the tabernacle.

[9] And it came to pass, as Moses entered into the tabernacle, the cloudy pillar descended, and stood *at* the door of the tabernacle, and *the* LORD talked with Moses. [10] And all the people saw the cloudy pillar stand at the tabernacle door: and all the people rose up and worshipped, every man *in* his tent door. [11] And the LORD spake unto Moses face to face, as a man speaketh unto his friend. And he turned again into the camp: but his servant Joshua, the son of Nun, a young man, departed not out of the tabernacle. [12] And Moses said unto the LORD, See, thou sayest unto me, Bring up this people: and thou hast not let me know whom thou wilt send with me. Yet thou hast said, I know thee by name, and thou hast also found grace in my sight. [13] Now therefore, I pray thee, if I have found grace in thy sight, shew me now thy way, that I may know thee, that I may find grace in thy sight: and consider that this nation is thy people. [14] And he said, My presence shall go *with thee*, and I will give thee rest. [15] And he said unto him, If thy presence go not *with me*, carry us not up hence. [16] For wherein shall it be known

here that I and thy people have found grace in thy sight? *is it* not in that thou goest with us? so shall we be separated, I and thy people, from all the people that *are* upon the face of the earth. [17] And the LORD said unto Moses, I will do this thing also that thou hast spoken: for thou hast found grace in my sight, and I know thee by name. [18] And he said, I beseech thee, shew me thy glory. [19] And he said, I will make all my goodness pass before thee, and I will proclaim the name of the LORD before thee; and will be gracious to whom I will be gracious, and will shew mercy on whom I will shew mercy. [20] And he said, Thou canst not see my face: for there shall no man see me, and live. [21] And the LORD said, Behold, *there is* a place by me, and thou shalt stand upon a rock: [22] And it shall come to pass, while my glory passeth by, that I will put thee in a clift of the rock, and will cover thee with my hand while I pass by: [23] And I will take away mine hand, and thou shalt see my back parts: but my face shall not be seen.

In this instance, as well as others (cf. Ex. 16:67,10; 24:16-17), God's glory had been seen through the agency of the cloud. Since the exodus from Egypt God had chosen the cloud as His means of limited revelation (cf. Ps. 18:11-12). It was the cloud that God sought to keep the people from breaking through as He descended over Sinai (Ex. 19:12-21) and in a thick cloud that God would meet them *above the Mercy Seat* (Lev. 16:2). Now, with Moses looking into the cloud, God spoke with Moses **face to face as a man speaketh to a friend** (v. 10). In later scripture, using an idiom that expressed an intimate and direct communication, it is said that God spoke with Moses *mouth to mouth*, while he (Moses) beheld a *similitude of the Lord* (Num. 12:8). Recognizing the degree of intimacy and revelation that had been afforded Moses gives greater clarity to the request of **shew me thy glory**. Simply put, Moses was asking for what his dispensation could not allow; God's glory without the agency of the cloud.

Recognizing this, gives greater clarity to the request of Moses when he petitioned God, **shew me thy glory**. Moses was asking what his dispensation could not allow. He was asking to see God without the veil of the cloud. This of course could not be accomplished **for there shall no man see me and live (v. 20)**. To remedy this impossible request, God said that he would pass by Moses, who would be hidden within a cave covered by the hand of God. After God had passed by in all His glory, then and only then, God would allow Moses to look into the residue of His passing (called the hind parts). This brings to light the incredible dynamics of what it was to see Jesus Christ, whom scripture reveals, was *the fullness of the Godhead bodily* (Col. 2:9). In the New Testament, God was no longer veiled behind the obscurity of the cloud. Jesus was God in flesh (cf. II Cor. 5:19; I Tim. 3:16), totally man and totally God, *the brightness of his glory, and the express image of his person* (Heb. 1:3). According to John's Gospel, when Christ came, *we beheld his* (God's) *glory* (Jn. 1:14). No longer God hidden in a cloud but now God revealed through humanity, whose ultimate purpose was to relationally right humanity to Himself so that He could once again dwell in the midst of His people, only this time, in temples not made with hands, but rather, within the lives of blood-bought, water baptized human beings, through the indwelling of His Spirit as seen in the Book of Acts (Acts 2:1-4, 38).

Notes

CHAPTER 34

¹ And the LORD said unto Moses, Hew thee two tables of stone like unto the first: and I will write upon *these* tables the words that were in the first tables, which thou brakest. ² And be ready in the morning, and come up in the morning unto mount Sinai, and present thyself there to me in the top of the mount. ³ And no man shall come up with thee, neither let any man be seen throughout all the mount; neither let the flocks nor herds feed before that mount. ⁴ And he hewed two tables of stone like unto the first; and Moses rose up early in the morning, and went up unto mount Sinai, as the LORD had commanded him, and took in his hand the two tables of stone.

Hew thee two tables of stone like unto the first: here, unlike the first instance where God had hewn the tablets, Moses would now be held responsible to provide the stone that God would etch the commandments upon. Interestingly, it would appear that the tablets Moses provided had been hewn at the foot of the mountain and brought up to God the next day. Indeed, the weight of those newly hewn tablets must have weighed heavily upon the ascent of Moses to renew the covenant with God.

⁵ And the LORD descended in the cloud, and stood with him there, and proclaimed the name of the LORD. ⁶ And the LORD passed by before him, and proclaimed, The LORD, The LORD God, merciful and gracious, longsuffering, and abundant in goodness and truth, ⁷ Keeping mercy for thousands, forgiving iniquity and transgression and sin, and that will by no means clear *the guilty;* visiting the iniquity of the fathers upon the children, and upon the children's children, unto the third and to the fourth *generation.*

Here what is commonly referred to as the 13 attributes of God is articulated as God passed by within the cloud. These attributes are still recited during Jewish festivals and other holy days among orthodox Jews. Interestingly, though the mercy of God is being established, God reiterates that His mercy will in no means clear the guilty. In other words, as a merciful, gracious, longsuffering, abundantly good and true God, the impenitent will still receive justice and judgment.

⁸ And Moses made haste, and bowed his head toward the earth, and worshipped. ⁹ And he said, If now I have found grace in thy sight, O Lord, let my Lord, I pray thee, go among us; for it *is* a stiffnecked people; and pardon our iniquity and our sin, and take us for thine inheritance.

Moses' haste is couched upon the recognition of the condition of the people of God and, as such, he petitions God to consider his own position with God. Moses' appeal will be that God go among the congregation of Israel by considering the relationship he has with God. He, like many other of the prophets, claims the iniquity and sins of the whole, begging that God pardon iniquity and sin and take the children of Israel as an inheritance.

¹⁰ And he said, Behold, I make a covenant: before all thy people I will do marvels, such as have not been done in all the earth, nor in any nation: and all the people among which thou *art* shall see the work of the LORD: for it *is* a terrible thing that I will do with thee. ¹¹ Observe thou that which I command thee this day: behold, I drive out before thee the Amorite, and the Canaanite, and the Hittite, and the Perizzite, and the Hivite, and the Jebusite. ¹² Take heed to thyself, lest thou make a covenant with the inhabitants of the land whither thou goest, lest it be for a snare in the midst of thee:

¹³ But ye shall destroy their altars, break their images, and cut down their groves: ¹⁴ For thou shalt worship no other god: for the LORD, whose name *is* Jealous, *is* a jealous God: ¹⁵ Lest thou make a covenant with the inhabitants of the land, and they go a whoring after their gods, and do sacrifice unto their gods, and *one* call thee, and thou eat of his sacrifice; ¹⁶ And thou take of their daughters unto thy sons, and their daughters go a whoring after their gods, and make thy sons go a whoring after their gods. ¹⁷ Thou shalt make thee no molten gods. ¹⁸ The feast of unleavened bread shalt thou keep. Seven days thou shalt eat unleavened bread, as I commanded thee, in the time of the month Abib: for in the month Abib thou camest out from Egypt. ¹⁹ All that openeth the matrix *is* mine; and every firstling among thy cattle, *whether* ox or sheep, *that is male*. ²⁰ But the firstling of an ass thou shalt redeem with a lamb: and if thou redeem *him* not, then shalt thou break his neck. All the firstborn of thy sons thou shalt redeem. And none shall appear before me empty. ²¹ Six days thou shalt work, but on the seventh day thou shalt rest: in earing time and in harvest thou shalt rest.

²² And thou shalt observe the feast of weeks, of the firstfruits of wheat harvest, and the feast of ingathering at the year's end. ²³ Thrice in the year shall all your men children appear before the Lord GOD, the God of Israel. ²⁴ For I will cast out the nations before thee, and enlarge thy borders: neither shall any man desire thy land, when thou shalt go up to appear before the LORD thy God thrice in the year. ²⁵ Thou shalt not offer the blood of my sacrifice with leaven; neither shall the sacrifice of the feast of the passover be left unto the morning. ²⁶ The first of the firstfruits of thy land thou shalt bring unto the house of the LORD thy God. Thou shalt not seethe a kid in his mother's milk. ²⁷ And the LORD said unto Moses, Write thou these words: for after the tenor of these words I have made a covenant with thee and with Israel. ²⁸ And he was there with the LORD forty days and forty nights; he did neither eat bread, nor drink water. And he wrote upon the tables the words of the covenant, the ten commandments.

²⁹ And it came to pass, when Moses came down from mount Sinai with the two tables of testimony in Moses' hand, when he came down from the mount, that Moses wist not that the skin of his face shone while he talked with him. ³⁰ And when Aaron and all the children of Israel saw Moses, behold, the skin of his face shone; and they were afraid to come nigh him. ³¹ And Moses called unto them; and Aaron and all the rulers of the congregation returned unto him: and Moses talked with them. ³² And afterward all the children of Israel came nigh: and he gave them in commandment all that the LORD had spoken with him in mount Sinai. ³³ And *till* Moses had done speaking with them, he put a vail on his face. ³⁴ But when Moses went in before the LORD to speak with him, he took the vail off, until he came out.

And he came out, and spake unto the children of Israel *that* which he was commanded.

Moses' encounter with God caused an unforeseen side-effect, unbeknownst to Moses, in that his face shone קָרַן (*qāran*), meaning to *radiate light* (cf. Hab. 3:4). Having been in the proximity of God's glory, including the experience of peering even into the hinder parts of God, Moses' face reflected the fundamental nature of God's glory; light. The motif of light throughout scriptures is commonly connected with God and those that are of God's nature. Consistent throughout scripture, God's glory is often described as a brightness (cf. Ezek. 1:28; 10:4) and a light (Isa. 60:1, 19). God is said to dwell *in the light which man can approach* (I Tim. 6:16). This idea continues in the New Testament, whereas Jesus was explained as being the *brightness of his glory* (Heb. 1:3). The further motif of light is found in those who are called *out of darkness into his marvelous light* (I Pet. 2:9), called also the *children of light* (I Thess. 5:5), which was made possible through the infilling of God's spirit, as evidenced in Acts 2:1-4, where Luke described what seemed *like* ὡσεί (*hōsei*) *tongues of fire* upon each of those who had received God's Spirit. The likeness of fire would have served as a 1st century simile to describe the unfolding fury of light, paralleling, in some fashion, the experience on Mount Sinai when God's glory descended in the cloud (cf. Ex. 24:17), now having fallen upon those in the Upper Room.

[35] And the children of Israel saw the face of Moses, that the skin of Moses' face shone: and Moses put the vail upon his face again, until he went in to speak with him.

That is to say, when Moses finished speaking, he put a veil on his face so *that the children of Israel could not steadfastly look to the end of that which is abolished* (II Cor. 3:13). Moses clearly sought to ensure that the children of Israel would never see the glory fade from his face during periods of time marked by God's communication to the people. Moses' words carried the impact of evidence that he had indeed been in the presence of God.

Notes